"Kinetic Life *contains the road map for unleashing full potential, which is first based on clarity of purpose, passion, and goals. Melerick Mitchell provides perspective and practical skill-building to generate the life you desire—and will aspire to. Well done!*"

—*Stedman Graham*
Speaker, Author, and Entrepreneur

"Kinetic Life *emphasizes the power of mentorships and, to my delight, highlights the diversity of a young woman in STEM. This book reveals a concise process to achieve your goals in a highly engaging and relevant way. Bravo, Mel!*"

—*Yolanda Lee Conyers*
Vice President, Worldwide HR, and Chief Diversity Officer, Lenovo

"Kinetic Life *will elevate mentoring from merely being an overused buzzword to a truly practical application and systematic process of development.*"

—*Dan Gilmartin*
CFO, Meeting Professionals International
Former CFO, Color Tile, and President and COO, Frank's Nursery and Craft

"*Via* Kinetic Life, *Mel has outlined an invaluable step-by-step blueprint that helps you maintain the courageous agility to achieve levels of impact of which you've only dreamed. It will*

literally change your relationship with the phrase 'what is possible.' Read it. Take copious notes. Then reread it again!"
—Karan Ferrell-Rhodes
Founder and Chief Differentiation Officer, Shockingly Different

Kinetic Life *is a transformative and practical parable for any reader needing courage and a process to take action. Mel's systematic coaching framework has guided me to unearth my passion and purpose, and propelled me to pursue my life's audacious goals.*
—Lacie Pierre
Management Consulting, Accenture

This book resonated with me at many different levels: the deep conversations, the authentic mentor-mentee relationship, and the compassion for the 'greater' good pretty much sums up my relationship with Mel. He provides a very simplistic approach on how to find your inner voice, focus on your passion and purpose, and continue your journey through life. I have been able to apply these principles through my personal and professional 'roller coaster' and I have come out on the other side stronger and even more driven.
—Rutu Patel
Technology Adoption and Communication Manager, Alaska Airlines

KINETIC
Life

UNLEASH YOUR POTENTIAL

Melerick H. Mitchell

ISBN: 0985510250
ISBN: 9780985510251

To Hannah and Preston: May your roller coaster of life lead you to your audacious dreams and goals. Uncle Mel is paving the way for you.

Contents

Acknowledgments

First and foremost, I must thank God for ordering my steps and placing me on my current journey. It is only because of His blessings and grace that I have had the life experiences, ideas, and opportunity to create *Kinetic Life*.

The creation of *Kinetic Life* was a true team effort. The Kinetic Life team—consisting of Suzanne Leonard, Patrick West, Kendrick Carroll, and Alex Canales—is one of the best teams I have been on. Suzanne and Patrick, you guys *ROCK*. You gave life to my words, concepts, and ideas, and having you two on the team elevated the quality of the content in *Kinetic Life*. Kendrick, thank you for your patience while designing the cover of *Kinetic Life*. You listened to our suggestions and nailed the design for the cover as well as the other diagrams. Alex, your work on www.Kinetic.Life and the supporting structure has provided the backbone for creating the Kinetic Life community.

To my fellow authors (it feels great to be able to say that) Brent O'Bannon, Tiphani Montgomery, and Kristin Andress, thank you for taking the time to share your writing and publishing best practices with me. The insights I received from all of you made this journey easier.

I could not write about mentoring and achieving life's audacious goals without recognizing four individuals who have provided mentorship and guidance to me over the past two decades. Thank you, A. C. Hollins, Chris Fernandez, Mario Pipkin, and Ron Johnson. Your consistent encouragement and advice has helped me successfully navigate my life's roller coaster.

As always, a special thank-you goes out to my core support team: my brother, Raamel, my parents, Melvin and Bobbie, as well as my girlfriend, Adrianne Prysock, for all the encouragement and support over the many months it took to complete this project. I could not have done this without your support.

Overview

You want to be part of something larger than yourself. You have a desire to be successful and achieve your dreams. You're not alone.

Those desires are something we all have in common.

Unfortunately, the majority of us fall short of achieving our dreams and goals. There are a number of reasons why this occurs. For some it is the combination of roadblocks, distractions, and fears that derail them, and for others it is a struggle to understand their purpose and recognize their dreams.

After having the privilege to coach and mentor hundreds of people, ranging from students to CEOs, a pattern emerged in those who experienced a higher rate of success. The people who are more successful have a greater level of clarity about their motivations. They know what is required to achieve their goals, and above all they have the courage to take action. Based on these coaching sessions, extensive research, and applying a little science, specifically physics, *Kinetic Life* was born.

Kinetic Life is a systematic process that will enable you to achieve your audacious goals in life and equip you with the tools necessary to push through the resistance you will encounter on the journey. This book will help you have a life that is full of passion, purpose, and direction, but first you must take the steps and actions required to align your heart, head, and body with your goals and dreams.

During the research phase for *Kinetic Life*, I studied several books on leadership, coaching, and life planning. While most books were written in the traditional nonfiction or training format, the books that had the greatest impact were written in a parable format. This led to the decision to write *Kinetic Life* in a story format for the reader, as it is a fast read and easier to apply to real life.

The *Kinetic Life* story has been written from both the mentee and mentor perspective to help anyone who has an interest in growing their own skills and developing future leaders.

Mentee: Someone who is in search of or pursuit of a specific goal or dream.

> I encourage you to engage with the text by taking notes and completing the homework posted at the end of each chapter. By doing the homework along

with the characters in the story, you will reap the benefits of creating a life plan to conquer your audacious goals and achieve your dreams.

Mentor: Someone who invests his or her time to develop the next generation of leaders.

We all have the power to change the world, and it is our responsibility to do so. A proven method for implementing positive change is mentoring. Good mentoring relationships have the ability to bless both the mentee and the mentor.

As a mentor, you are encouraged to use *Kinetic Life* as a guide to help your mentees achieve their goals in life. Feel free to use the examples and coaching points in this book in conversations with your mentee.

This book is divided into four parts:

Part I—Heart: Focuses on raising your potential by utilizing the elements of your heart, which are passion, purpose, and audacity. You will create a foundational road map that is required to achieve your audacious goals and dreams.

Part II—Head: Concentrates on accelerating potential by leveraging your focus and thoughts so that you can identify the knowledge, network, and level of influence required to take action.

Part III—Body: Guides you in transitioning from your potential state to being Kinetic so that you can move toward your desired reality.

Part IV—Staying Kinetic: Outlines how to maintain and leverage the momentum you have created and overcome the challenges, roadblocks, and detours that you will encounter on the journey.

A *Kinetic Life* quick-reference card is included at the end of this book.

Your Kinetic Life begins the moment you take action toward your audacious goals and dreams. You must always remember that life is an activity, and to get the most out of life you must fully participate. While participating in life, there will be resistance and setbacks. You will need energy to achieve the reality you desire, because there are no free rides, but it's good to know that that you will get out of life what you put into it.

Our goal together is to unleash the freedom of time and energy by living a Kinetic Life. This new reality will allow you to invest yourself meaningfully, and on purpose, in those things that matter the most.

Let us embark together on this great journey to discover your new reality of living Kinetic.

Introduction

Will and Alexis

"**A**lexis is a warrior. She is unyielding, focused, and relentless. Over many years of service alongside her, I have witnessed the warrior in action, and I assure you it has been a sight to behold. Her combination of grace, dignity, and compassion for humanity has fueled her into battle time after time. She has been a true champion of our organization's mission, the eradication of type 2 diabetes. We attribute our many successes to her commitment."

"Wow! Look at you, getting honored for your roller-coaster ride," Will whispered, sitting at the head table to Alexis's right. He gave her one of his familiar crooked smiles. "Alexis, you have come a long way. Oh, and"—he nudged her with his elbow—"thank you for being seen in public with me." They both laughed at the longstanding joke between them.

Soon the introduction ended and her moment arrived.

The applause was muted behind the sound of her heartbeat and the click of her heels as she made her way onto the stage. Her eyes adjusted to the glare of the spotlight, and the voice inside her head became silenced in the embrace of a longtime friend and champion who was introducing her.

She smiled and tried to shake off the feeling of embarrassment from the public display of compliments. Her mind wandered into its own inner monologue: *Am I really all those things? Well, I'm not afraid and I care deeply about the millions of lives diabetes has impacted. They deserve warriors on their behalf.*

As quickly as she became lost in her thoughts, she just as swiftly hit her stride on the acceptance speech. Alexis poured her heart out before them in a battle cry for more warriors to rise up and step into the fray. The standing ovation was a brilliant moment for her, as she had led them to it for the greater mission.

■ ■ ■

Alexis had developed a distinct appearance that embodied a yin-yang of contributing cultures. Her parents were both first-generation immigrants, her father from Mexico and her mother from India. In some places that might seem an odd combination, but in Seattle cultures have mingled and evolved due to corporations with diverse employment and communities that embrace diversity.

Growing up, she found that being a free spirit in this environment was easier than being bound by cultural or social restraints. She preferred being active in causes over ball games, dances, or parties. Her studies often took a back seat to her passion for helping others. But when she did make her education a priority, she was an exceptional student, especially in math and science. This was a constant concern for her parents and led to numerous dinner-table lectures about "seizing the great American opportunity." Deep within, she knew they were right.

Late in her senior year of high school, Alexis decided to pursue marine biology. For her parents, the excitement of learning she had finally made a decision was short-lived. They wanted her to pursue accounting or engineering. She didn't reveal her feeling that she was not fully confident in her decision (what eighteen-year-old is), but she made it anyway.

Living around Puget Sound and the Pacific Ocean played a role in the decision, because it had piqued her interest in the environment, animals, and the vast unknown lying beneath the waves. The discoveries and possibilities seemed endless. Despite the fact that many of the cool kids were heading into this major, she was going to beat them by taking it seriously.

Her studiousness didn't immediately overwhelm her desire to help others. It was in her third year of college that the free spirit within her began to mature, by choice and also by circumstance. She started to see the world quite differently.

One evening near the beginning of her junior year, her father called to tell her he was laid off from his job. The news shook the foundation of her world. While she had earned a scholarship for books and had grants and loans for tuition, his financial support was needed to cover her living expenses. Losing his middle-class job meant the sacrifices would run incredibly deep.

With her adrenaline pumping, Alexis packed her computer in the apartment she shared with two other girls and crossed the street to her favorite neighborhood coffee shop.

Unlike most days, this wasn't a time to study. Today would require planning and looking through job sites to find out what she would qualify for at this stage in her life. Her work experience had primarily been as a volunteer, although in high school she had had a couple of short-term retail jobs. She wondered how she would parlay her limited experience into a real job that would pay the bills. The search quickly turned the situation into a sudden, harsh, and overwhelming reality. She sunk her head in her hands and quietly the tears began to fall.

The tears may have fallen quietly. They didn't fall unnoticed.

The coffee shop's owners watched out for the students in the neighborhood. This provided a sense of family and home for the community, no matter how far from their actual families they were. When Alexis walked in that afternoon, they knew something was not quite right. Her usual bright spirit was missing and she went straight to a table in the corner. When her head sunk into her hands, Martha looked at her husband, Roland, and they nodded in agreement.

Roland rounded the table and sat directly in front of Alexis, taking both of her hands in his. "Alexis, why do you cry?" She let out a final sob, squared her shoulders, and accepted his handkerchief to dry her eyes. "There is nothing in this world you can't handle. Tell me what is going on and let us see if we make sense of all this crying." His second-language enunciation of English words always made her smile. It reminded her of home and calmed the torrent.

Forgetting the demands of his business day, he sat patiently and listened to her. Roland and Martha built their business on caring more about people than money, often saying, "Investing in people takes time." In this case, there would be an immediate return on these values.

Roland had just learned that one of his top baristas landed a job at Boeing and would be leaving. Holding onto his surprise for her, Roland asked Alexis, "Do you like coffee?"

She looked into her cup. "You know that I do."

He leaned in to catch her distant stare. "Do you like people?"

She accepted his eye contact. "I love serving people." Her shoulders sank a bit more as she exhaled the words.

"Alexis, we just had a position open up. Randy has landed that"—he waved his hands in the air—"dream job with Boeing. We need someone as soon as possible, and you look like the right person to me."

It took a moment for Roland's words to sink in. "Really? I don't know what to say, I'm so excited…I'm…" She quickly moved around the table and, without considering that this was her soon-to-be boss, threw her arms around his neck and thanked him over and over like a young girl would her father.

Settling back in her chair, squaring her shoulders, and regaining her composure, except for the gigantic smile across her face that gave it all away, she replied, "Thank you. I accept." Without resume, application, or interview required, she had a job. A great job.

He looked up as if to say thank you to God and leveled his eyes back on her. "This is lesson number one for you as an employee here. If you keep your eyes on what is most important, and here in our shop it is the people, everything else, like problems"—he waved his hands in the air again—"will solve themselves."

That evening she called her father with the news. It was tough for him to learn that she had accepted a job, as it was a point of parental pride to financially support her through her educational years. Her mother, on the other hand, was relieved, and Alexis enthusiastically shared the full story with her of how it had come together magically, as though it was a divine plan that was working itself out.

Alexis worked at the coffee shop and put herself through college. She graduated with a bachelor's degree in marine biology. Her excitement to begin a career in the field was unfortunately met with challenges that were outside of her control. The industry had few jobs and an abundance of experienced biologists already in the field. She was unable to land a job, and the temporary job at the coffee shop became her full-time work.

Over time she expanded her experience by taking on every possible managerial role at the coffee shop. Refusing to give up on her dream, she continued to take college courses in various areas of the sciences. She also maintained her involvement in causes she loved, mostly with school-age kids and in the sciences. Despite her growing experience and managerial skills, she still found this to be a very hard and uncomfortable place to be, and, as she learned to her dismay, it's not an uncommon tale.

■ ■ ■

One rainy Tuesday afternoon the coffee shop was quiet when John Henderson, a friend who led several of her labs at the college, stopped by to see her. John shared the same love for science that she did; however, he was well ahead of her in the master's program in biomedical engineering. She took a coffee break to visit, and they settled in the back corner away from the customers.

"What brings you to my neck of the woods?" Alex was playing the role of straight shooter, but the evidence that she was kidding came through her eyes.

He crossed his arms and leaned across the table as if to share a secret. "I am here to recruit you to the dark side." They both laughed. "Honestly, I would like to invite you to volunteer with me at TAF's annual conference next month. It is here in Seattle, and a few of us are getting involved in their projects and events."

Alexis had always been passionate about TAF, the Technology Access Foundation, a nonprofit leader in science, technology, engineering, and math, commonly known as STEM. Based in Seattle, TAF equips students of color for success in life through the power of a STEM education. In high school, she had attended TAF workshops and labs, and later gave back by volunteering as a lab assistant in its junior high school programs.

Alexis knew the national TAF conference was coming up, and if she attended she could meet people in her field from around the world. This made her beyond excited and was the opportunity that she really needed. Her words poured out in a flood. "John, you are awesome! Yes, of course I'd love to help. When is your next meeting? Do I need to register anywhere? I need details!"

John had graduated from the TAF Academy and went decisively into his major, which she envied now more than ever given her current circumstances. In the flood of excited words, she also confessed her envy and revealed her concerns about her current predicament. When she shared more about her situation, he inquired, "Have you thought about getting a mentor?" She loved the idea but didn't know where to start.

"My mentor, Will McDowell, will be at the event. His company is a financial contributor to TAF, and he has worked for major corporations as an engineer. It's really cool that he now owns a firm that consults with businesses on how to develop their leadership pipeline. Hey! I'll arrange a meeting for the three of us. He would know where to start. I bet he also has access to great mentors who are seeking mentees."

Alexis was exceedingly grateful to John for the suggestion, but most of all for offering her what might be the huge break she needed.

■ ■ ■

On the day of the event, Alexis jumped right in as a volunteer at the youth exhibits. This allowed her to work with the young people as a mentor. By serving in this way, she became convinced that a mentor was exactly what she needed to answer the difficult questions and overcome the challenges ahead of her.

The week of the event was a well-engineered storm of activity. She met many leaders she had read about or had watched online, and it was exhilarating. She asked lots of questions about how they came to their specific fields of expertise and absorbed any advice they could give her. It was obvious that the leaders were there to pass on their wisdom to the next generation, which was evident in their eagerness to answer questions and engage the potential of young people. They genuinely seemed to value their role as mentors. With all these great leaders present and their positive feelings about mentoring, Alexis hoped that John's mentor would be able to help her get plugged in with one.

They planned to meet in the convention center's café for a quick coffee between meetings. John would be unable to join them, as she had been hoping, due to a last-minute conflict. She was on her own. Nervous for the meeting, she arrived early and passed the time by checking her social media feeds on her tablet.

Engineers are notorious for punctuality, so when Will arrived a couple of minutes late, he was in an obvious hurry and apologetic for keeping her waiting. He was not what she had expected. From his online profile, she expected him to have a personality a little more Dr. Sheldon Cooper from *The Big Bang Theory* than what she saw, Denzel Washington meets Vin Diesel. On first impression, he was a cool guy and very approachable.

"So John tells me you studied"—he paused to recall—"marine biology?" Alexis nodded and somehow forgot to speak in her nervousness. "What made you pick that major? Do you like working in your field so far?" Unknown to Will, he had just jumped right into her sea of troubles.

"Yes. Well, no. Actually, that is where I find myself today. I can't find a job in my field. I'm feeling pressure due to the money I spent and still owe for my degree, and"—she pressed through her insecurity toward humor—"with all this water around us, you'd think I could find a job around here." She looked down at her hands fidgeting with the corners of her tablet. He asked for it and pulled a stylus from his pocket.

"It seems you are right where we all have been at one time or another. We have the potential to go in different directions, but choosing can be difficult. Let me show you something that might help."

She nodded her head, and this time remembered to speak. "Sure."

Will drew a line up a big hill, down the hill, and halfway up again. "This is what I call the Roller coaster of Life. Everyone is on the roller-coaster ride at one place in the process or another." Will paused in reflection while drawing the image.

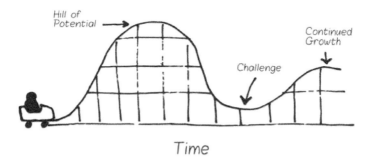

"Interestingly enough, it was an actual roller coaster that started me on my journey into engineering. I was a kid in the sixth grade and we were headed on our final field trip to Six Flags over Texas. The trip was like our rite of passage into junior high. The 'get outta here, you're done' celebration." Alexis smiled as she recalled her own final field trip in elementary school. "I could not wait to experience being on my own for a full day at an amusement park. Most of all, I wanted to ride the roller coasters. We all saw the TV commercials for the newest ride, Shockwave, and it was definitely my favorite. It took you up a huge hill to gain the kinetic energy required to launch through the two loops, twists, and turns.

"The first time I rode it, I was nervous and perhaps a tiny bit scared. In my heart I felt excited, alive. I mean, come on, this was a whole lot more exciting than riding my bicycle at home." They both laughed. She was now glued to his story. "When you think about riding a roller coaster, it involves your entire being. During the ride, we experience it in our heart, head, and body. As the coaster is pulled up that first big hill, our heart is full of enthusiasm, nervousness, passion, and excitement. We look down the tracks and try to prepare our body for the experience. But it's during the ride that our heart and head are telling our body when to throw our hands up and when to hold on tight. It's this incorporating our body in the experience that makes the ride complete for all of our senses.

"Pursuing our goals in life is very similar to riding a roller coaster. There are ups, downs, twists, turns, and at times we are even taken for a loop. So shouldn't we expect that on the roller coaster called life we would experience similar effects to our heart, head, and body?"

She understood where this story was going. "Yeah, I can see that. Life is like a roller coaster." She thought back to when her father lost his job and the sudden g-force from the loop that required her to change direction and find employment.

"It is. Now, my love for engineering came from learning the mechanics of the roller coaster. It is based on simple principles of physics: potential energy, kinetic energy, and momentum. Even more than that, I found that these principles can also be applied to our lives.

"So, to nerd out a bit, you understand that the energy you invest in building your potential is required before you can take action. That energy will be converted to kinetic energy when you begin to take action toward your goals. This is possible because of the law of conservation of energy. Energy can be neither created nor destroyed, it only changes states."

She thought about that for a couple of moments. "Of course I understand the theory, but I'm a bit confused as to how this will"—she exhaled, feeling a bit defeated that it didn't all make sense—"help me make the right decision for my life right now."

"Don't worry. We're heading there. Let me expand on this." Will pointed to the first hill in his diagram. "Just like on a roller coaster, we must build our potential before we can take substantial action toward our goals. To begin that process, the first hill we must conquer is the 'hill of potential,' and this hill is often the steepest, highest, and takes the longest time to climb. During that climb we are continually building our potential to take decisive action toward our life's aspirations. Summiting this hill requires consistent input from our heart and head. However, the foundation for our potential is our heart: it contains our passion, purpose, and audacity. When these elements combine, they act as a motivational engine for the climb. While our heart provides the required motivation for the initial movement toward our life's goals, our head delivers the necessary focus and thoughts needed to achieve those goals. As we combine the forces in our heart and head, our potential increases, which prepares us to become kinetic."

Alexis looked at the first hill and quickly realized that she was at the beginning of her climb up this hill of potential. She leaned in over the diagram as if she was asking for more. Will answered the unspoken request. "As we summit the hill of potential, our body kicks into gear and we transition from the potential state to the kinetic state. Becoming kinetic enables us to take action. This action provides the momentum and force required to take us over and through the twists, turns, and loops we will face as we push toward achieving the audacious goals we have set for ourselves."

She sat back in her chair and looked up. "So what you are saying is, I will get out of it what I put in, and there will come a time that the investment will become energized, kinetic, taking me where I want to go in my life and career?"

He smiled. "Yes, that is exactly what I am saying. You will find a life full of passion, purpose, and direction once you take the steps and actions to align your heart, head, and body so that you can have a kinetic life."

She took a breath and shook her head. "I still don't know where I want to go."

"That's OK for now. Lao Tzu said, 'A journey of a thousand miles begins with one step.'"

She instantly knew her first step. "Mr. McDowell, I know you are mentoring John, but I would like to know if you could take some time with me to learn this process. I want to make a difference in this world. If I become kinetic, just think of what I could accomplish for the good of humanity and, well, be happy doing what I love. I know I have a long way to go, but I'd like to know if you could mentor me."

Will pulled a business card out of his pocket. "I can. Here is my card, and I'd like you to email me next week so we can set up next steps. I'd be happy to take you on a great journey to discover your new reality of having a Kinetic Life. The freedom of time and energy will allow you to invest yourself meaningfully and on purpose in those things that matter the most to you. Welcome to the ride, Alexis. Get in, buckle up, and keep your hands and feet inside at all times. Remember, you are tall enough to ride this ride!" They both laughed. "Together, let's write your next chapter."

Alexis left the café in a state of awe and wonder. She headed back to the exhibit hall with a new perspective and sense of urgency to learn more from Mr. McDowell, her new mentor! Her stomach quivered with excitement and she skipped a few steps in celebration.

Part I
Heart

CHAPTER 1

Passion

Roller Coaster of Life

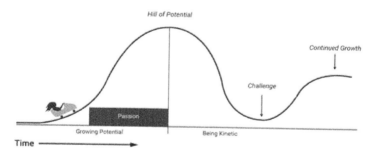

The week following the conference, Will was back in his Dallas office preparing for a multicity trip that was to begin the next day. He had handled nearly all the follow-ups from the conference but one item, an e-mail he had just received from Alexis.

Mr. McDowell,

It was great talking with you at the TAF conference last week and I hope the rest of your visit
in Seattle went well.

I was really intrigued by our conversation on
the roller coaster of life. If your schedule allows,
could we meet over the phone one day next week
for our first session?

Thank you again for agreeing to be my mentor.
Sincerely,
Alexis

Will smiled, thinking back on all the mentees in his life and
where they were now. Mentoring had become something
that gave him great joy. Alexis was one he felt had great
potential and once empowered, there was no telling how
far she would go. Before leaving the office, he took his last
minutes to respond.

Alexis,

Great meeting you too, and I'm happy to be
your mentor.

Would next Tuesday, June 12 at 4:00 p.m. work
for you?

Will McDowell
Founder and President
LeaderTech, Inc.

Alexis didn't realize she was holding her breath while
opening the email. Her gasp drew unexpected looks from

her classmates. She blushed and repositioned deep in her chair to appear smaller. "I still can't believe he said yes," she whispered at the email on her phone.

She quickly hit reply to confirm, and hesitated while her mind swirled with doubt. "I don't know what I want to do anymore. I'm just out of college and still working in a coffee shop. He's the president of his own company. Will this be a waste of time for him?" She shook the doubt away and courageously hit the send button.

The day of the call came, and anxiety was on the menu. She swallowed her nerves and dialed. He answered on the second ring as if he were patiently awaiting her call. This surprised her, as she had prepared her professional voice for his administrative assistant to answer.

"Mr. McDowell, this is Alexis. Thank you for scheduling this time with me today."

Will quickly replied, "It's my pleasure, and please call me Will."

She made the decision to be transparent with him right away out of respect and concern for his time. "Thanks again for agreeing to be my mentor. This is a first for me and honestly, I am not sure how this works, but I am willing to learn."

The inflection in her voice gave away her uncertainty. He reassured her. "Alexis, I have faith that you will learn and grow from the process. I am committed to helping you discover your purpose and value, and as your mentor it is my responsibility to help you avoid the mistakes I have made." His word of commitment was all she needed.

"Before we get started, I want to go over a few simple rules. Sound good?" Alexis cheerfully agreed. "Mentoring is a relationship, and it only works if both parties are fully committed to participate. As a mentee, your first commitment is to schedule our meetings. I look to you to keep track of the action items we discuss and to follow through on them. You must do what you say you will do, because our conversations are not just about having a motivational dialogue, but about me helping you achieve your goals. This will take action on your part. Do you agree to this?" His tone was serious but kind.

"Yes, I agree."

"Good, I also encourage my mentees to take notes during our sessions. We will cover many areas swiftly and you will have great revelations that you need to capture. So feel free to use any note-taking method that works best for you. You can record our sessions, type notes on your computer, or take the old-school approach of handwritten notes.

"For me, as your mentor, my responsibility is to coach, guide, and push you to stretch and grow. At times I'll share stories about my past, or how I view a particular topic. Other times I'm going to ask you tough, thought-provoking questions to make you think. Always remember that this is all done so that you can achieve your audacious goals. Are you OK with this structure?"

"Yes. I like stretching my mind and being pushed to achieve more. That's one of the things I liked about my teachers and soccer coaches growing up. They always pushed me to reach for that higher rung."

"Good to know. Alexis, we talked briefly at the conference, but tell me a little more about yourself. Where are you from, what do you like to do, and why did you choose marine biology as your major?"

"Well"—she paused, not sure exactly what he'd really want or need to know—"I was born and raised in Seattle. My mom is from India and my dad is from Mexico City. Growing up around these two very distinct cultures has given me a passion for international work, although I haven't done much of it." She stopped to hear what she had just said, "passion for international work," and scribbled it on the paper she had pulled out when he was going over the rules about taking notes. "I have always liked helping people most of all. I volunteered a lot in high school but find it harder to do now between my classes and full-time job." She made another note: "Help people. Volunteering."

"You are currently working and going to school?"

She thought about the situation that pushed her into employment. "Yes, well, I had to get a job to cover my living expenses." She didn't reveal why, out of respect for her father. "And I really like it. I am a barista at my favorite coffee shop, and now, since graduating, I'm taking on more responsibility. It's like I get paid to spend time with all my neighborhood friends and make up crazy concoctions that taste good and make people smile." He quickly picked up on her good attitude about having to work while in school. It was a very good sign.

"So you are a mad coffee scientist–slash–social butterfly?"

She giggled a bit and wrote down his words. "I guess you could say that. I must have changed after high school, because I wasn't very social back then. I was quiet and liked to spend my time solving problems for people, not going to dances." She paused and wrote down "problem solving."

"How did that lead you into marine biology?"

She looked down at her paper and wondered the same thing. "I lived near the water all my life and I feel connected to it. I love science and biology specifically, so I guess it just felt right." She wrote down "science and biology." A knot formed in her stomach. She wasn't on the right path and wanted to shift the conversation away from her for a moment. "Will, I looked up your bio and was wondering what made you want to leave a career in technology to start a business that focused on teaching leadership? It is so different."

"Great question, Alexis. Growing up, I always had a passion for math, science, and technology. But at the same time I also had a knack for getting along with almost anyone because I just liked people. I think that is something I got from my parents." He paused in reflection. "When I was a kid, I could always organize a group of kids to do something. Whether it was building a clubhouse in the woods or forming a team to play sports after school, getting people together around a goal just came naturally to me. Over the years, I grew that gift into a skill for developing people, leaders, and teams. That natural gift has now become a full-blown passion. So in the technology field, I found that my passion for organizing people around projects and goals was stronger than it was for directly creating the technology. For me it was a natural transition. It was a bigger hill of potential to climb, but one I was very passionate about, and it energized me." This made Alexis reflect back to her childhood from a different perspective.

"This brings us back to passion, the first building block. Do you still have the roller-coaster diagram I sketched out for you?"

Alexis quickly took another note, "changing direction is OK." She pulled out her tablet and switched it on. The sketch was already on her screen from looking at it prior to the call. "Yes, I have it right here."

"Good. We talked about the hill of potential that you are climbing now. Passion is the fuel to get up that hill. It is one of the key driving forces in our lives. Our world is shaped and moved by those who live with passion. So, Alexis, tell me, what are you passionate about?"

She looked down at the words she had written down. "There are a lot of things that I would say I'm passionate about." She was subconsciously mounting her defense in choosing marine biology. "Are you asking about work, school, or things I like to do with my personal time?" She secretly hoped he wouldn't say school.

"Great question. It could be any of the areas. For our mentoring conversation, let's focus on the one you see at the top of your priority list based on the stage of life you are currently in."

The ball was to her toe and she couldn't avoid it. "Right now I see myself in the learning phase of life. So I guess the right answer is marine biology?"

Will let out a small chuckle. "Alexis, you have come up with a technically correct answer. But what is it about marine biology that excites you? What about it stirs your soul and makes you come alive?"

There was a long silence that he intentionally didn't interrupt. "Those are some pretty deep questions. I've never thought about it that way. It reminds me of a line in a movie I watched over and over again as a little girl, 'It's got to be that can't-eat, can't-sleep, reach-for-the-stars, over-the-fence, World Series kind of stuff, right?'"

He laughed. "Well, I told you that my role is to ask you the hard, thought-provoking questions. Seems we have already touched on a difficult area for you, and that is OK. It reminds me of the great philosopher Henry David Thoreau, who at twenty-eight years old went into isolation for two years to write books. In the first one he wrote: 'I went to the woods because I wished to live deliberately, to front only the essential facts of life, and see if I could not learn what it had to teach, and not, when I came to die, discover that I had not lived.... I wanted to live deep and suck out all the marrow of life.'

"I keep that quote on my desk because it conveys the passion of a man who wasn't skating through life, he was instead pushing all limits."

When he said that, she realized she couldn't honestly answer the question regarding her passion for marine biology and felt deflated. "Will, I used to feel passion for marine biology, but I am having a hard time finding it now. I feel that it is changing direction for me, and I am sorry to say this, but I don't know what direction I am going in and until I do, how can a mentor help me?" This came from the depth of her tortured soul. He acknowledged the trust she was extending and her honesty. He told her encouragingly that this honest assessment was a breakthrough to celebrate.

Will committed the rest of their time to helping her identify her passion. He took her through a series of questions that started with things she likes to do. "We can often find our passions in the things we do every day. Alexis, what activities energize you and what do you get out of them? Does the enjoyment you get out of them make you feel as if they have elevated your life to new heights?"

Alexis went to her notes. "I love being a mad coffee scientist! I create drinks with chemical components that make your taste buds do a happy dance. I think this qualifies as a bridge between engineering and biology. But I really love volunteering. It is all I have ever wanted to do with my free time. To help another person or make a situation better by solving a problem gives me a level of happiness I can hardly define." She went on to talk about the desire to work internationally and her newfound social skills.

"This leads us to my next questions for you. What are your top gifts, talents, and skills? How are you using these talents?"

She looked down again at the words she had written earlier in the conversation. "Well, I find science and biology come very easily to me. Since elementary school I have always gotten good grades and loved the classes. Then, when I was in high school, a movie came out about a team of biologists who built a prosthetic tail for a dolphin. It was so inspirational, and come to think of it, that was why I finally chose to go into marine biology. I know that I have a gift for solving people's problems and I had been using that skill when volunteering, but I wanted to use it to help animals and the environment."

"Alexis, you have shared some very compelling attributes about yourself. Can you tell me what are the common denominators in these lists?"

She looked down at the lists. "Yes! I see them!"

No matter how many times Will took his mentees through this process, the aha moments never grew old. "OK. Let's make a list of these and prioritize them."

After reviewing the list, they realized that solving problems, studying science, and helping people were Alexis's top passions. Will asked her to come up with a passion statement and she did: "I am the happiest and most fulfilled when applying science to solve problems and help those in need."

"Alexis, this is a breakthrough. You started out apprehensive, but you had the courage to press on. Excellent work! Now, I want you to think more about the questions and bounce the passion statement off some people in your circle of influence for feedback."

She eagerly agreed. "Thanks again, Will, for taking this time out of your day to meet with me. If it's OK with you, can we schedule our next meeting in two weeks at the same time?" He was encouraged by the proactive stance she took and agreed to a time.

As she hung up the phone, it dawned on her how comfortable the conversation had become. It wasn't like talking to a friend at the coffee shop or a family member. It was different: purposeful, intentional, respectful. She really liked being mentored.

Passion – Homework

- What activities energize you?
    - What do you get out of them?
    - How do they elevate your life to new heights?
- What are your top gifts, talents, and skills?
    - How are you using these talents?
    - What are the common denominators among them?
- Create your passion statement.

Notes:

_____

_____

_____

_____

_____

_____

_____

_____

_____

_____

_____

_____

_____

_____

_____

_____

_____

_____

_____

_____

CHAPTER 2

Purpose

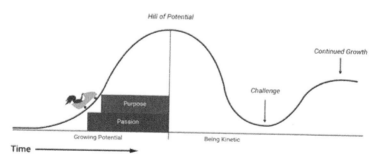

Roller Coaster of Life

Hill of Potential

Continued Growth

Challenge

Purpose

Passion

Growing Potential

Being Kinetic

Time

O ver the next two weeks, Alexis discovered that she naturally became energized when talking about passion and all she had learned. She shared the results of the first mentor session with her family, her boss, and John, her fellow mentee and the friend who had introduced her to Will. Their responses were empowering. They agreed that it accurately defined her spirit and passion. It was as if she'd aced the test, and she was excited to move on to the next level.

With this first step covered and a full tank of fuel to climb her hill of potential, she dialed Will for their second mentor session.

"Good afternoon, Will. How is it going today?" She was excited about the call but tried to calm her voice.

"It is going very well, Alexis. What about you?"

She took a deep cleansing breath. "I'm very excited to share the results of our last meeting." Alexis jumped right in. "I spent time thinking about my passion and took your suggestion to bounce it off people in my life, one of them was John. While my parents were very happy to see the results and my boss agreed it summed up my talents, when I talked to John about it he kind of laughed and asked me more questions."

She could hear the smile in his voice. "Excellent! I am glad to hear that he pushed you even harder. What type of questions did he ask?"

Alexis couldn't remember exactly but summed them up. "He asked me what five words describe my burning desire in life and what I'd want to be known for. The five words were helping, people, solutions, science, and hope. But what I want to be known for? All I could answer was that I want to apply my talents in making a difference that help as many people as possible." She heard her words and felt sheepish for a moment and tried to backtrack. "Sounds kinda silly now that I hear it."

"Alexis, that is not silly at all. What you just shared is your heart. The heart is where the truest form of passion resides. You just connected your head to your heart. This is a very good thing. Did this change your passion statement?"

Alexis felt at peace in her soul that she was on the right track and boldly shared her new passion statement. *"I'm passionate about solving problems and implementing solutions that help people."*

"I'm glad to hear you have gained this level of clarity on what you are passionate about. With this passion statement, what do you believe you should do with it? What type of problems do you want to solve?" Alexis was quiet. The wheels in her head were on overdrive because this very question was what she was struggling to answer, and Will picked up on it after the pregnant pause. "The reason I am asking you this is that for you to continue on your ascension up the hill of potential, you have to know your purpose. Knowing your purpose is a vital key to applying your passion to help people in a very big way. When you have this understanding of your purpose, it will ground you because it comes from a deep belief in your soul. It is why you have the passion you do. It's the intersection between your passion and your purpose. This is where you'll discover your authentic self."

Alexis liked the "why" axis in his guidance, but she was still unsure of her own. Will continued. "Let's lay a little groundwork here. Before you can uncover your purpose, we must take a look at how your passion relates to your core values. You see, our values provide the foundation for how we live, act, and behave. Let me give you an example. It is not uncommon to see parents work second jobs to send their children to better schools, because as parents they believe in the value of education."

"I totally get it, parents who work extra jobs so that their kids get a good education, because it is something my father believes in. But do you have other examples?" She was straining to fully understand.

"Yeah, no problem. This is not a personal example, but have you ever heard of the company Zappos?"

She giggled a bit. "Yes. I ordered a pair of shoes from them once."

"Well, Zappos is a great example of a company whose success is directly linked to its values. In 1999, Nick Swinmurn and Tony Hsieh had the audacious goal of creating a different type of company, so they set off to first build a unique culture. If you do a little research, you will find it well documented that by defining, communicating, and ultimately embodying their values, they successfully established this very different culture. I've visited the company many times with teams who are examining how they too can differentiate themselves by committing to live by their mission and values. Zappos is the very best corporate example of this."

"Didn't that go viral? I thought I saw a speech on it once. It seemed really cool, because their employees were not the usual corporate suit-and-tie people, they were all very different. I remember liking what I saw." Her inner millennial spirit was connecting to this story.

"Yes, it did. Tony wrote a book, and there was quite a bit of coverage on this story. But what made it so unique was that they were delivering WOW in their customer service, which is the first of their ten values. You have to understand that during this time, many companies were being efficient with customers and these guys wanted to be effective. So, if a call took five minutes or thirty-five, all that mattered was that the customer was wowed by the service. If in the end it didn't go well with the customer, the reps could send a gift of cookies or flowers."

"Seriously? The employees could send a gift to someone who was unhappy? That seems crazy. I've never heard of a company doing that."

Will smiled. "Well, this company does it. From the moment you walk through the front door, examples of their mission and vision are everywhere. Even their ninety-minute tour is a 'wow'-ing experience.

"So you see, Alexis, the question here is not about what you do, it is again why you are doing it. I want you to consider your values in several areas: family, faith, and career. Family is often an easy place to start, because your parents influence your values, so you would look outside yourself in order to look within."

She thought about her parents and sighed. They loved her so much and instilled so many good things in her, not just by talking about them, but in their actions. "My parents have taught me so many great values. I think about school and how my dad's high standards for me taught me to have those high standards for myself. He taught me to never give up but keep working at things, hard things, until I did them. My mom, on the other hand, taught me to be a woman of my word. If I said I would do something, then I had to be organized to ensure that I did them."

Will looked down at his notes. "So what I am hearing you say is that they taught you to be diligent and disciplined, while requiring excellence from yourself?"

She typed the three words into her notes. "Yes, exactly! But when I think of my parents, the first thing that comes to me is a warm feeling of love. You see, they are so kind to everyone, and their journey to create a new life in the United States makes me so hopeful for my journey in life.

"But you said faith, and when I think of faith I think of God. My parents raised me mostly Catholic from my dad's side of the family, and my mother is nondenominational Christian, even though she was raised in a Hindu culture. My foundation is based upon my faith in God, and I believe that He wants good things for me. He wants to help me live out my purpose on earth."

"So hope, love, and kindness describe your faith values?"

She was amazed he picked them up so quickly. "How are you reading my mind?"

Will let out a laugh. "Alexis, you are saying these words. But keep in mind that I have also studied values and the hundreds of words used in value statements. If you are interested, you can go online and study the lists of words that are out there."

She was tempted to look immediately but resisted and made a note instead. "Great! I will do that."

"Good. So, I'd like you to do the same exercise regarding your career using those lists. Think about Zappos and their search for the 'why.' You might also want to look up a video called 'How great leaders inspire action.' It's a viral video that talks about the power of 'why.' Once you get all your words together, I'd like you to write down your 'why' for each of your values. Finally, you will write down the talent or gift you have that comes from that value and why."

Alexis was thankful she was recording the session, because those were serious instructions he was giving her. "OK, um, let me see if I understand what you are asking for. So one value for me is kindness. It is important to me because, as my mom would say, sugar catches more flies than vinegar. Basically it is important to consider someone else's feelings and needs as you would want them to consider yours. The talent or gift…I can't seem to come up with more than 'I am kind.' I care about what people need and find myself listening often so I can maybe help solve their problems."

Will jumped in to pull it together. "So your value is kindness. Your why is that people's well-being matters deeply to you, and your gift is listening. Alexis, that gift can be developed into a great talent, a critical talent toward your success. If you can stay in tune with people by not simply hearing them but truly listening to them, you will have greater control over the management and outcomes of all the situations you encounter in life. This is a great gift that you should focus on developing."

He paused for a moment to speak to someone in his office. "Alexis, I am sorry, but we will need to wrap up a little bit early today, something has come up here in the office. How about you work on those values and we reconnect in about a week's time? Shoot me a text to this number and we can go over it."

Despite her disappointment, she responded kindly, "Sure. I will do that. Thank you!"

Alexis went to work on her values. She researched on the Internet and found videos that helped her understand what values are and how to connect them to her gifts and talents. It was not long before she began to see her passions come alive in her own values, and she took great pleasure in journaling about them. She wrote about interactions and activities over that week and captured pages and pages of thoughts that helped her uncover the answers on her own within the words, just as Will had done. Instead of always listening to others, she was now hearing her own voice.

The day came to text Will. She had reduced a couple of dozen values down to six and wrote the why and talent for each one.

Alexis texted: Good afternoon, Will. I am checking in with my answers to the homework.

Will responded: Hello, Alexis. Great! Tell me what you came up with.

Alexis: This is the summary of my answers: Education, the key to success and future, math and science. Faith, we are here for something greater than ourselves, grace. Hard work, to earn the things you want in life, enterprising. Challenge, makes me feel alive, problem solver (math and science). Intelligence, go beyond smart, applied knowledge.

Compassion, able to help more by feeling what others feel, humanitarianism.

Will: Excellent work! Those are very insightful answers. I'd like to hear more about them. For now, pull out your passion statement and look at these answers. I want you to write your purpose statement using the passion and values. Remember, your purpose isn't necessarily work-related. It is what you feel strongly about and moves you to becoming a better you.

Alexis: Can we meet again next week on Tuesday?

Will: Sure. Let's do 3:00 this time.

Alexis: Yes. Thank you!

Referring to her notes, Alexis went back over everything she had written to come up with her purpose statement. She thought about the word "purpose." The definition is "the reason to exist," which is heavy but didn't feel heavy to her. She was now pretty confident she understood her 'why' and started writing.

On Monday, the day before their next scheduled meeting, Alexis couldn't contain herself anymore and sent Will a text:

Alexis: Will, sorry to bother you but I'm really excited about my purpose statement and wanted to share it with you: I believe we all are entitled to live a healthy life, and I want to create medical devices that help people live full lives.

> Will: Again, Alexis, this is incredible work. I agree with this and look forward to talking more about it tomorrow. Thank you for sending this to me. It brightened my day!
>
> Alexis: Thank you, and yes, I am looking forward to tomorrow. BTW, looking at my purpose I'm thinking about going back to school this fall, and if I do I will be choosing a different major. ☺

Alexis set her phone down, closed her eyes, and envisioned this new path. It excited her greatly to share it with Will, but this also meant she was responsible for seeing it through. She would also have to consider that she would have to make another investment in her education to move into this new career path. As she sat quietly, her inner self was at great peace with the first of many decisions she would be making.

Purpose – Homework

- Identify your top values.
  - What is your 'why' for each of your values?
  - What is your talent or gift that comes from that value and why?
- Create your purpose statement.

Notes:

_____

_____

_____

_____

_____

_____

_____

_____

_____

_____

_____

_____

_____

_____

_____

_____

_____

_____

_____

CHAPTER 3

Audacity

Roller Coaster of Life

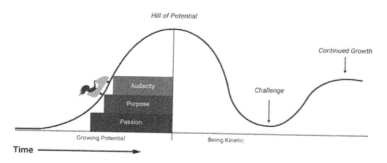

"Good afternoon, Alexis. Since your text yester-day, have you thought any more about what you are going to major in when you go back to school?"

Alexis had begun to anticipate his nudge toward next steps, and she was proud to be a step ahead. "Yes, as a matter of fact. I talked to several of the deans at the university about my passion and purpose. They helped me by going over the classes I've taken and those I will need to get the right degree for this kind of work. We narrowed it down to mechanical engineering and biomedical engineering. I'm personally learning toward biomed."

"Excellent! Both are good majors that will provide you with a lot of career options. Now, before we dive into your audacious goals, I wanted to say that I really like your purpose statement. I know you have a passion for math and science, but I was wondering what made you want to shift into creating medical devices."

Alexis paused to gather the answer in her head and heart. "I have been doing research on type 2 diabetes over the past week, because my cousin was diagnosed with it several years ago, and her condition has begun to worsen. The more I read on the condition…well, it's really sad to me. Millions of people are impacted by it, and I think I can make a real difference in their quality of life."

"Based on that comment, I think you will really like today's conversation. But first I want to point out that you have also chosen an area that has a very high demand for talent like yours. This means more jobs are available and you will have more options and greater security in your career."

She hadn't thought of that. "Now that you say that, it makes sense. OK well, I'm ready to take the next step on my hill of potential!" There was great excitement in her voice on continuing along this path of self-discovery, which always pleases a mentor.

"Well, OK Alexis! Let's keep moving up the hill on your roller coaster. The next step is audacity. I'm curious, when you think about audacity, or audacious goals, what comes to your mind?"

She thought about it a moment. "I guess I think of people or companies that are pursuing some type of big dream, like an Elon Musk."

She was unsure about the answer and surprised by his response. "You are right on point. People and companies that change the world start out with, and continue to have, big, audacious goals. For us to begin defining these goals, an audacious mindset is required. I'm sure you can see that through the lens of this mindset your goals would be based on your passion and purpose, representing the change you are striving to make in your life right now. Just looking at the word 'audacious,' you have to know that these goals are in no way going to be small or simple. Instead they're bold, original. They defy normal convention. They're uninhibited and so big they almost scare you. Despite this fear, your heart feels a rush of excitement, because they are exciting! This is the *you* that's in your heart. That place deep within your heart is where your audacious goals reside. From that place, you have the power to shake and change our world, Alexis. You are familiar with Microsoft, right?"

He shifted the conversation, and she felt a rush of adrenaline. "Living in the Seattle area, who isn't? Actually, a couple of my older friends were in their IT Rotation Leadership Program. It seemed really cool how the company moved them around to learn about the different parts of the business." Will smiled, as he had consulted the company on this program, and he was surprised she had heard of it but moved on in the lesson.

"We have seen this kind of audacity play out in the way Paul Allen and Bill Gates approached the computer industry in the mid-1970s. At that time, the computer and technology industry looked vastly different. If you wanted a personal computer, you most likely had to build it from scratch, meaning you had to actually build your own motherboard. If you worked for a large corporation, it might have a few computers, which were primarily used by engineers and data processors. But they believed that computers would change the world. From that belief they launched Microsoft in 1975 with the audacious goal of seeing a computer in every home and office running Microsoft's software, and it wasn't by chance that they ventured into the computer industry. These guys had been working together developing software as a hobby for several years, and during that time became experts.

"But for Gates and Allen to achieve their audacious goal, two things had to happen first: the distribution of personal computers had to increase, which was starting to occur at that time, and, more important, they had to build a team of software developers and engineers to create the software to power the computers. These initial developers had to have the same insane passion for technology and strong desire to change the world. Forty years later we see the results, as we have computers not just in every home and office, but in our hand as smartphones, in our cars, powering our home entertainment systems, and even on our bodies to manage our health and wellness."

His rhythm shifted and he became assertive. "Alexis, the pursuit of audacious goals is not for the faint of heart. To achieve your life's audacious goals requires a serious gut check. You must understand that in striving to attain your goals, you *must* be willing to push through pain, setbacks, rejection, hurts, delays, and self-doubt. However, it is possible if you maintain a can-do attitude, with grit, tenacity, toughness, and, most important, faith in your journey, along with an unwavering commitment to the ride."

Alexis felt what he was telling her deep in her chest. It was not going to be easy, but she wanted that level of audacity in her goals, in her life.

"So, Alexis, based upon your passion and purpose, what big change would you like to make in the world? Keep in mind that the impact you desire to make could be personal-, family-, or community-focused, something in business or a change you want to make in the world."

There was laughter in her words. "Funny you should ask me that. Our sessions have started me thinking a lot about my goals and the impact I want to make. I think about it when I am reading and researching the treatment of diabetes. I know researchers are making great strides in developing devices like pumps to treat those on insulin and also prosthetics for those who have lost limbs. I believe I can contribute to moving the development of those devices forward. With that being said my audacious goal is to revolutionize the technology and devices used to treat diabetes."

Will leaned back in his office chair and nodded his head in affirmation. "That's what I'm talking about. That, Alexis, is a swinging-for-the-fence type of audacious goal!"

Alexis immediately came back with, "Well, you know me. I'm a swinging-for-the-fences type of girl!" Laughter erupted between them in celebration of this breakthrough.

"You remind me of a Walt Whitman quote: 'The powerful play goes on, and you may contribute a verse.' You have been blessed with a great heart and the intellect to back it up, Alexis. I believe you can achieve that audacious goal and absolutely contribute your verse."

Alexis believed him. She could achieve the goal, but she must fully apply her talents to the mission of building her potential and then hold on for the roller-coaster ride. "Will, I am committing myself to this journey. What is next?"

He liked her tenacity in applying the teaching and her eagerness to start the ascent up her hill of potential. "Well, it seems to me that the target audience would be those with diabetes. But is there a larger group that would benefit from your attainment of this audacious goal? Would your work help others?"

She pondered that a few moments. "I have noticed that my cousin's diagnosis and treatment plan has impacted not just my cousin directly, but her entire family. It has been very emotional and scary at times, especially when she went into hypoglycemic shock and was unresponsive. They thought she had died. So the targeted audience should include people with diabetes and their caregivers?" She answered her own question: "The solutions should take all those impacted into consideration by giving them better ways to manage the disease and also the other health complications." It was obvious she had been doing a great deal of research and was already becoming a living factbook on the topic.

"That sounds like a very holistic approach, and I agree with you. Now, your audacious goal is solid, but I always like to push my mentees to kick their goals up a notch or two. So, looking at your goal, how would you finish this statement: 'This goal would be even greater if…'? What would that 'even greater if' be?"

"Since type 2 diabetes is often preventable, it would be better if I could help people not get the disease in the first place. Perhaps I could help lead campaigns that would increase awareness of type 2 diabetes so that they will not need my technology?"

He immediately saw the power in this statement. "I have to point out what you just suggested. You wish to serve humanity with integrity and are willing to devote yourself to these advances while solving the very problem that creates the demand for your devices."

Alexis felt sheepish that she had not seen the error in her goal. "Oh wow, um, I hadn't thought of that."

Will let out a small laugh. "This was not a correction. I am pointing out something I find remarkable in the millennial generation. You see, there has been much debate around health care and the commercial economics of health care. What you said shows that your generation, but most important, you, have the natural tendency to do what is right over what makes business sense. It's as if you see the greatest good in all things. I don't care if they call it seeing the world through rose-colored glasses. I think it's awesome. It is a powerful character trait that will serve you very well, my friend."

It felt like a loop on the roller coaster, from thinking she was going in the wrong direction to being back in the right direction in the blink of an eye. "You know what? I think you are right about my generation. Most of my friends talk about how we care about things, the things we feel matter over the things that just make money or are in the best interest of the few. Unfortunately, I feel the world doesn't understand that. It's like you just said, it can be a very good thing! Just depends on who you are talking to, I suppose."

"Yes, that is a very big subject that we will take up sometime. For today, we have covered some serious ground. How do you feel about the progress we have been making over the past couple of weeks?"

She couldn't believe he was asking her this. "Are you kidding me? I now know my direction! I feel like I'm moving toward getting into my zone, if you know what I mean. I'm excited and have confidence in the decisions I've made in the process. Thank you so much, Will!"

He let the moment wash over him and understood this was exactly why he mentored. "I know exactly what you mean, Alexis, and you are very welcome. I'm glad you are finding our sessions beneficial. So, let's recap. Based on our conversation today, have you decided what you are going to major in this fall when you return to college?"

After a slight pause Alexis said, "Biomedical engineering."

"Excellent, great choice. You will do well in that field. Now, for homework, I'd like you to print out your passion, purpose, and audacious goal and frame them. Put them where you can see them every day. Move ahead with the university to get set up for this fall session, as it is about four weeks away."

She hadn't grasped that it was coming up so quickly. "Oh yeah, I need to get classes scheduled." She sighed. "And I need to figure out how I am going to pay for it. I can't keep working full time and it's too late for grants. I guess I will have to look into loans this semester."

"I'm a businessman and I know a good bet when I see it. This will be a worthy financial investment, even if the capital comes from a loan. I have confidence in you. This leads us perfectly into our next session. We've worked through what is in your heart, and we will move on to work on what is and will be in your head through all this education you are gaining. You must next learn how to focus."

They said their goodbyes, and when Alexis put the phone down she took in a fast breath of anxiety. There was so much to do, yet she felt energized to get it done. It was amazing to be in this flow. She jumped to her feet and ran to print her Kinetic statements. Realizing she didn't have a frame, she went online to get creative ideas. There she found a website that showed how to create a vision board. This was very intriguing, because there were so many exciting things rolling around in her head that she didn't want to forget, and this looked like a great way to capture them. She grabbed her keys and headed to the store to get the supplies for her project.

On the way, her phone rang. It was her mother. She had been so consumed by the process that she hadn't called home in a week! This was not good, but now she had to speak with her parents about her new plan to go back to school. In a split second she decided to get more information on loans first and then go home to discuss it with her father. She answered the phone with the goal of making plans to have dinner with her family in a couple of days.

Audacity – Homework

- What is the big change or impact you would like to make in the world?
- This goal would be even greater if _____.
- Print your passion, purpose, and audacious goal. Place them where you will see them every day.

Notes:

_____

_____

_____

_____

_____

_____

_____

_____

_____

_____

_____

_____

_____

_____

_____

_____

_____

_____

_____

Part II
Head

CHAPTER 4

Focus

Roller Coaster of Life

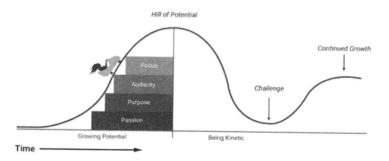

I t was hard to believe that in a short six weeks so much confidence and clarity had emerged. Alexis was focused on the next steps that would take her into this new stage of life. Her heart and head were pointed in the same direction and the enthusiasm and energy were unlike anything she had experienced before. She liked feeling in control of her future.

Alexis arrived at her parents' home for dinner with this renewed confidence. She prayed that her father would bless her decisions. As she came through the front door, the wonderful smell of home and her mother's cooking provoked a sense of melancholy. So much had changed in her life since she had lived here, but it always felt so good to come home.

The dinner table was set when she arrived, and after hugs of welcome they sat down to enjoy the wonderful family feast. She looked across the table at her mother and saw sadness in her eyes. Her father seemed tired, which was understandable, as his new job required him to travel around the city for onsite meetings.

She wondered if her news would brighten their spirits. So, she jumped right in. "Mom, Dad, I have some news for you." Her mother had a look of concern and her dad made an all-too-familiar face, as if he was readying himself for a blow. "I have decided to move into a new career path and I will be returning to college in three weeks." She paused for a reaction, but they both just stared at her. "You see, the mentoring I've been getting has helped me see my future clearly. So while I have been working on my passions, purpose, and goals, well, it has led me to make this decision to go into biomedical engineering. The reason I arrived at this is the research I have been doing since Devi's diabetes has gotten worse. I see the possibility of creating devices that help manage the condition, and I am also interested in prosthetic advances—"

Her prepared speech was cut short as her mother began to cry. "Sweetheart, that is so wonderful." She looked at her mother, dumbfounded. This was not news to cry over. Her father interjected, "Alexis, we just found out that Devi has been scheduled to have her right foot and ankle amputated. The neuropathy has created a severe infection. They can't fix it."

Her body went cold. This can't be happening. Devi was only thirty-seven—too young, based on the statistics. Alexis's mind swirled from her knowledge of the disease to her childhood, when Devi was her favorite cousin and babysitter.

"I don't understand, how could this happen? When will she have the surgery?"

Her mother was beyond words, and again her father answered. "I am not sure how, but she is in the hospital now. They have tried to fight the infection in her foot, but it was not successful. She goes into surgery the day after tomorrow."

The drive home felt like a long, dark journey. She was able to briefly reassure her father about college and that she already set up the financial arrangements with a loan for the first semester and continued part-time work. He gave her his blessing and full support. It seemed the timing of the news about Devi and her choice of a career collided that night. She knew it was a sign.

■ ■ ■

"Good afternoon, Alexis. How are things going? Are you still having fun as the mad coffee scientist?" She could hear the playfulness in his voice. The mentor relationship had turned the corner into a comfortable friendship that Alexis had grown to depend on.

"Ha-ha! Yes, I am."

Will sensed something in her voice right away, as she exhaled sharply. "So you're all set to get back to school next week?"

Her enthusiasm was flat. "Yes. The loan covers tuition and books with a little extra to live on. I'm registered for two physical classes, two online classes, and one lab, for a total of thirteen credit hours. I will continue at the coffee shop part time. I met with my parents and have their support."

Her thoughts trailed off to Devi. Seeing her after surgery was heartbreaking. Devi was amazing about the whole thing, but the family was deeply suffering. Finally, Will broke the long silence as her mind wandered into this other part of her life. "Alexis, is everything OK? You don't seem yourself."

Alexis shared what had happened to Devi. It felt like a sign that she was headed in the right direction with her career. They took a little time to talk about what she experienced and how it impacted her focus on the goal.

"Do you have the diagram of the roller coaster?" She did. "You can see on the hill of potential we covered the first three building blocks, passion, purpose, and audacity, which completes the section relating to the heart. Now we will start to discuss focus and influence, which have to do with the head. I do need to let you know that I have a hard stop at four o'clock because of a meeting with my business-coaching group. I call them my informal board of directors; they have been really helpful to me over the years in solving various business problems. Today I have a couple work issues that I need advice on."

"Wait, hold up. I thought once you are boss you no longer need a mentor or coach." He could hear the youth in her voice.

"Even as a leader, one thing remains true, you never have all the answers and you can always learn from other people. What I find helpful about my coaching group is that they help keep me focused on my main passion. It's like the saying 'As iron sharpens iron, so does one man sharpen another.' My coaching group has certainly helped me focus on being a better leader, manager, and husband. This leads into today's topic of focus."

"Focus. I don't have a problem focusing, because it comes easy for me. All I have to do is focus on my school-work and my work at the coffee shop. I've got this, everything will be good." Thank God they were on the phone, or he would have seen her roll her eyes.

"Hold up! Slow your roll, girl." They both laughed. "Actually, the level of focus I'm talking about is a more all-encompassing focus. The reason is that where we place our focus determines our thoughts, our thoughts determine our actions, and our actions determine our reality. If you want to change your reality, it all starts with where you place your focus. If you want to achieve your audacious goal, then focus is going to be required."

Her reply was a curious "Humph."

"A couple of years ago, my brother, Malcolm, who is big car enthusiast, asked me to join him in NASCAR racecar driving experience at the Texas Motor Speedway. In this experience, you have the opportunity to drive an actual racecar by yourself without an instructor." Will was intentionally shifting the tone of the conversation, and it seemed to work.

"Sounds like a fantasy camp for adrenaline junkies!" Alexis quipped.

"Oh, it is. When you arrive at the track, you are first given a racing suit to wear, and then you head over to orientation with all the other drivers. In the orientation session, they walk you through where and how to drive your car on the track, which was very important, because if you are too high on the track you will hit the wall, too low and you could spin out. In addition to the driving instructions, you learn about the safety features of the car in the event you have a crash.

"Once orientation was completed, we headed over to the track to wait in line for our car. While waiting in line, I started blocking out all distractions, because this wasn't a time to be thinking about email, social media, work, or anything else but driving.

"When my car arrived, I buckled up in the five-point harness, plugged my headset into the intercom so that I could hear the instructions from my spotter, and then got in the zone to be totally focused on the task at hand, which for me was to drive this car as fast as possible. While in the car, I placed my attention on only three items, the line my car took on the track, the rpm of the car, and the instructions the spotter was telling me over the headphones.

"As I pulled out of the pit row, my spotter instructed me when to merge on the track and where my rpms should be. As I entered each turn, he would give me feedback on my approach and where my rpm should be. After that, he instructed me to increase my rpm, so that on each lap I went faster and faster while remaining focused on the same three items. Once my time was done, my spotter told me to pull the car into pit row. I was very ready to do so, because driving a car at a hundred fifty-four mph requires an enormous amount of focus and concentration.

"From this experience I learned two things. First, good coaching can help you go faster. Second, focus is required to achieve your goals, which led me to think about what would happen if I applied the same level of focus and concentration on my goals daily. For me to do this would be what Jim Collins calls applying the hedgehog concept. This means to focus only on the things that will lead you toward achieving your primary mission."

Alexis asked, "So what you are saying is, I'm the driver and you are the coach?"

He had her attention back. "I am one of them, absolutely. So now let's apply the NASCAR focus experience to our daily life. I apply four steps: first, identify my primary goal or understand how this goal aligns with my audacious goal; second, outline the most important items to focus on; third, remove distractions; and fourth, find support to help me achieve my primary goal. If this list makes sense to you, let's go through them. We will discuss each one briefly, and then for homework you can dive more deeply into each one."

Alexis was glad she was recording the call. He was going through things quickly. "Cool," was all she could muster to say amid her feverish note-taking.

"Last time we talked, your audacious goal was to revolutionize the technology and devices used to treat those with diabetes. So how does your goal of attaining a degree in biomedical engineering connect with your audacious goal?"

Hearing the goal after the week she just had felt like a having living purpose inside her spirit. "Well, I have to get the degree."

This was matter-of-fact. "OK. So over the next several years, what are the items you will need to focus on?"

She paused. "I will have to excel in the classroom, and in the office and labs."

"True, it is good to excel in the classroom and at work, but I want to challenge your definition of excelling. To me, excelling is beyond getting good grades or doing well at work. It is about raising the bar. To achieve your definition of excellence where will you need to place your focus?"

Alexis was quiet. "While you are thinking about where to place your focus, you might consider analyzing what your strengths and weaknesses are. Once you have done that, I recommend that you focus more on growing the strengths that will help you achieve your goal."

Her head was now spinning, he was moving through so very fast. "But what about my weaknesses, shouldn't I focus on making them strengths?"

He slowed down a bit, realizing he was cruising through the concepts swiftly. "Not really. It's good to know what they are so that you can mitigate their impact on your quest to achieve your goals. There are lots of online tools that can help you discover what those strengths and weaknesses are. I recommend Strengths Finder. I'll send you a link to my coach's site to take the assessment. I've used it personally and with others going through this process."

She made a note. "Cool. I will look it up."

"The next step is to remove distractions. What or whom do you need to remove so that you can focus on your top priorities? Take some time to think about what your top distractions are, their impact on your time and how you could negate their impact."

She thought a moment. "One of my big distractions is email and text messages from my friends. I also remember when I was working as a volunteer at one of the nonprofits a couple of years ago, it seemed like my whole time was spent replying to emails. I was not used to that."

"Yes, email can be a big monster, and it's a challenge for many people who work for me. If you like, I can send you the email management tips I shared with my team."

She giggled. "That would be great, an email on email management." He laughed at her ironic humor. "I also found that when I graduated and was unable to get on my career path, I would binge-watch television series. It's entertaining, but it definitely takes up a great deal of time. Facebook and Twitter are time monsters as well. Hmm, and I can't forget my two roommates. They always have some kind of drama. Come to think of it, this next semester I will need to find someplace away from the apartment to study." Her focus was back on the session.

"Good thinking. You need to designate a space for that focus and be mindful of those distractions you listed."

"I feel like I'm going to be too busy for it anyway. Plus, now I'm very focused on this audacious goal." There was truth to this and Will wanted to explore it, but he was in a battle with the clock, so he moved on.

"We also need support and assistance from others to achieve our goals. Who do you need to bring into your circle to help you focus? What type of mentor will you need to help you navigate biomedical engineering?"

She immediately replied, "Will, I thought you were my mentor. We're not done with our sessions, are we? I thought we still had many more to go."

"Alexis, no, we are not done. However, you need to understand that I'm a good mentor on items regarding life, career, and business, but I don't have expertise in the area of biomedical engineering. So it's good to connect with someone who knows the ropes in that area and can help you avoid the pitfalls many students fall into."

She was relieved. "That makes sense. What about John? He is almost done with his master's and certainly knows the ropes."

"That sounds like an excellent choice. I'd like to offer another suggestion for your circle to help you focus. You should consider joining one or two student organizations. Since I was an undergrad, I have been an active member of the National Society of Black Engineers. Being a part of NSBE has helped me immensely, because we were focused on excelling academically and succeeding professionally. So perhaps you might consider joining an organization like the Society of Women Engineers, the Society of Hispanic Professional Engineers, or the Biomedical Engineering Society." Alexis had been involved with a couple of the groups and committed to looking into the rest.

"We still have about ten minutes. Do you have any questions regarding any of the items we covered today or in any of our other sessions?"

She thought a moment. "I do. Even when I remove my distractions, I sometimes have a hard time getting into what I call the 'zone.' Do you have any suggestions on how I can do it better? Get there faster?"

"Sure. This took me many years to master. I would suggest that you make time in the 'zone' a priority. If you don't set this time as a priority, you are more prone to distraction. Choose a consistent time and location, because our mind and body works well with consistency. You will also need to outline a plan of attack before you start. Something that works well for me is when I'm finished working I'll spend five minutes outlining what I am going to focus on the next time. My favorite part is that I find a small way to reward myself for the work session. A reward process will help you make this a habit that you enjoy."

"Will, that is awesome! I have so much to plan over this week and hey, thanks, you have really helped me...focus. I have been really down and, I admit, off my focus." She nearly blushed at the admission.

"It is my pleasure, Alexis. All things happen for a reason, and this week has certainly brought you to a new level."

■ ■ ■

Alexis,

I enjoyed our conversation today, and as promised here are some tips on how to manage email.

In the workplace, email mismanagement can derail your productivity. The tips below can help you conquer the email monster.

8. Schedule a set time to read and reply to emails.
9. Handle each email message only once. If a response is required, then respond while you have it open. File emails that are for information only them in specific folder; delete all other emails.
10. Set email filters to automatically move emails to specific folders.
11. Use the phone. When you are pulled into a long email conversation, it is often quicker to pick up the phone and call the person.
12. Write well-formed emails. If you want someone to read your email, keep it short and to the point.

You can also go to www.gallupstrengthscenter.com to take the Strengths Finder assessment we spoke about today.

Thanks,

Will McDowell
Founder and President
LeaderTech, Inc.

Will,

I met with John, and he agreed to help me through the biomed engineering track! He will be a great resource for me. I told him we were working on focus and that strengths and weaknesses were my homework. He helped me narrow them down. Here is what we came up with:

> Strengths – Quick learner, hardworking, outgoing, courageous, follows through
> Weaknesses – Impatient, inexperienced, fear of mistakes, critical of feedback, perfectionism

I'm going to take the Strengths Finder assessment to see how it matches up!

Thankfully we have strengths on here, because I am not a fan of seeing any of my weaknesses listed. This must be my perfectionism coming out! I have also been so busy that my distractions haven't been an issue, there's no time for them to be. However, I did designate a well-organized space for focus time. I have not been able to get a schedule locked down yet for focus time, but that will come when things settle down. I look forward to our next session!

Thank you! Alexis

Focus – Homework

- What are your top five priorities?
- Identify your top distractions and their impact on your time.
- What or who needs to be removed so you can focus on your top priorities?
- Analyze how your strengths and weaknesses impact your focus.
- Determine who do you need to bring into your circle to help you focus?

Notes:

_____

_____

_____

_____

_____

_____

_____

_____

_____

_____

_____

_____

_____

_____

_____

_____

_____

_____

CHAPTER 5

Influence

Roller Coaster of Life

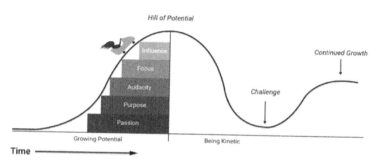

"Will, thanks again for letting me move our meeting time. I'm still trying to settle into a groove that balances work and school. I'm joining the Biomedical Engineering Society, and I met with them to see where I can plug in. Oh, and I'm also trying to help my family through Devi's amputation." She took a deep breath and realized that she was talking extremely fast and hadn't even inhaled yet.

Will couldn't see the flush of exertion on her face from her sprint home to be on time, but her hectic tone moved him to joke with her as she caught her breath. "No problem moving the meeting, and from your email I see that John is now on team Alexis."

She paced the floor in cool-down mode, and this comment tickled her with irony. "Yeah," she said, her reply filled with laughter, "team Alexis! Go, team, go!" She made cheerleading arm gestures to join the cool-down.

"I hear your winning spirit loud and clear!" He pulled the phone away from his ear as she cheered. "Alexis, you are in your second week of this new learning path and schedule, give yourself time to settle in. Rome was not built in a day, nor will you summit the hill of potential quickly. You are in the center of a transition period. Breathe and remember, you are tall enough to ride this ride! Hey, you mentioned Devi. How is she doing?" For Alexis, hearing this was like coming in for a crash landing.

"You know, it's really hard for everyone. She's always been like a big sister and role model to me. I would have done anything to protect her from this horrible disease. Her friends and the family feel the same way I do."

"Sounds like an incredibly difficult time that's just full of emotions."

She smiled at the thought that he could almost read her mind sometimes. "Yes, well, I got proactive and looked deeper into the various support services available for family members and friends of people with type 2 diabetics. I found a huge gap. It doesn't seem right, because I see it as a missed opportunity, for so many reasons." She exhaled. The cool-down worked and she sank into her chair.

"What do you mean by that? What is the opportunity?" Will's curiosity was piqued.

"Losing a foot is a very big deal. But the cause is actually the bigger deal. From what I have uncovered, the gap is around the education and support of family and friends upon diagnosis. There are various support groups and charities for traumatic events like an amputation. But wouldn't early education for type 2 diabetes have given my family the additional information they needed?"

Alexis paused before answering her own question. "I've spent so many hours doing research, and it seems to me that the point of diagnosis is the pivotal time to educate loved ones on the complex care, the risks, and preventing it for themselves. Let's face facts, families often share genetic and environmental factors that put them all at higher risk of getting the disease. You can't change genetic factors, but you can alter the environmental factors though lifestyle changes." She passionately tapped her finger on her desk as if pointing toward the truth. "It's those changes that set up promising conditions for people with diabetes to mitigate the horrifying results, like in Devi's case, an amputation. But what about blindness, kidney failure, heart attack, nerve damage? I don't know, it just seems so simple to me. So why aren't there more people focused on this bigger opportunity?"

"Great question," Will said. "It's because your purpose is to lead the way. Bravo, my friend. I do believe you took something in your life that was tragic and found your life's calling. It is truly inspirational, and seriously, wow! You now have tons of rocket fuel to propel through this season of learning."

Alexis' adrenaline rush came to a grinding halt. "Oh yeah, school. I really wish I had gotten it right with my first degree. I could already be working." She sighed audibly.

"But Alexis, all this brought you to a place where you feel alive with passion and purpose. Imagine if you had gotten another degree that led to a decent j-o-b. It paid the bills and you were OK with the day-to-day work. It could have been decades, if ever, before you discovered your true destiny."

She let that sink in deep in her spirit. He was right. Sometimes it takes the wrong path to lead you to the right one. Her voice was calm and measured. "Will, that is so true. Thank you for being in my tribe."

"I am honored to be in your tribe. It is quite the journey you are on. So, tell me, how is school going so far? Are you getting over all the barriers you had to deal with last time we spoke?"

Thankfully her tank was full of passion or the question would have launched her into another rant, "Yes, well, um, I sat in the financial aid office for what seemed like days. Actually, it was. I went three times and waited three, four, and one day six hours to see my counselor. I watched with envy as the students with their parents came in and out while I just waited. In the end, we got this semester covered and they said they would help me with next semester. God is good!"

Will smiled through his reply. "All the time. You certainly have been busy these last couple of weeks."

"Yes, it is all moving really fast. I'm excited to be back in school, but the thing is, I feel so much older than my classmates." She was edging toward regret again. "It is going to take me two and a half to three years to complete the degree. I will be twenty-seven years old when I graduate.

Twenty-seven!" She would not dare tell Will that she was secretly, yet unsuccessfully, formulating tactics on how she could shortcut the process and get around the degree.

"Let me ask you a question. If you do nothing for the next three years, how old will you be?"

This brought her out of her tactical daydream. "I will be twenty-seven." She felt sheepish bringing this up in the work session.

"Sounds like you are going to be twenty-seven in three years regardless, and if that is the case, you might as well have your degree at twenty-seven also!"

She surrendered. "You're right. I guess it's all just moving so fast, it makes me a little bit nervous. I'll just pull myself up by the bootstraps again."

"There is no such thing." His tone was forceful, but the underlying playfulness eased the sudden aggressive stance. "You may be tying up those boots, but you didn't make the boots. It is all a process, Alexis, and it takes a team, a tribe. You must build your support system and learn how to lean into your tribe for the help you need. You will not become successful by pulling up those bootstraps alone. That is what we are going to be talking about today. Deal?"

She enthusiastically responded, "Deal!"

"Great. So during our last session, we talked about where you were going to place your focus. Now we will discuss influence, which is the final step required in climbing the hill of potential. I love what John Maxwell says: 'The true measure of leadership is influence, nothing more, nothing less.' Understand that influence is our ability to drive a desired change. The greater our influence, the larger change we can potentially make. I say it this way,

'Little influence equals little change; large influence equals large change.' So your influence is the final step in converting potential energy into kinetic energy." Alexis was quiet as the wheels turned in her head.

"You might be asking yourself, 'Why is Will talking about growing my influence now? I'm just a barista and college student.' The reason why I wanted to bring this topic to your attention is because it takes time to develop this influence and to become a strong leader." Once again, he was in her head, and this time she felt exposed.

She stumbled over her words. "Yes, um, I was always led to believe that leaders are born. You know the saying, 'natural-born leader.'"

"There are character traits and talents that can predispose some individuals to become leaders. But leadership and influence are skills that can and must be developed. It's just like learning how to play the guitar. You might have a natural gift for music, but the more you practice, the better you will be."

"At this point in time, who am I responsible for leading? I don't run a company or charity. Heck, I'm not even the leader in my study group." She felt so small and sank down in her chair.

"These are very valid questions. Don't be discouraged. Do you want to know the key to this?"

She shook her head yes and mumbled, "Uh-huh."

"The most important person you have to influence and lead is yourself. If you cannot follow the directives you outline for yourself, how you can lead others?" This made sense to her. "Jeff Immelt, the CEO of GE, put it this way, 'Leadership starts with a contingency of one.'

"The key, if you want to be a good leader, Alexis, is that you have to lead yourself extremely well. In your case, leading yourself comes from how diligently you focus on your top priorities right now. Understand that people around you observe how you conduct yourself, and based on those observations, they will determine if they'll follow you beyond the positional power you might have today. So as your ability to lead and influence yourself grows, so does your sphere of influence. They are always watching. Oh, I nearly forgot to ask. Do you have access to your email? I sent you a diagram just before our call."

She reached for her tablet, which was recording the call. "Yes, hang on one second. Got it!"

He pulled it up on his computer screen. "Great. OK, this is what I call the Sphere of Influence."

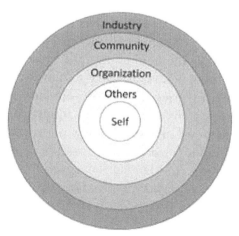

Sphere of Influence

"You see, it starts in the middle with what we just talked about, leading yourself first. Be influential with yourself. Trust yourself. Don't wait until you are promoted by circumstance or, in some cases I've seen, pure dumb luck. Be intentional in learning these skills long in advance. Alexis, I cannot stress this enough: you will not grow into a successful purpose-driven leader by accident." He took a breath to let it sink in. "Now, do you see that being at the front of the line or having a big title doesn't make you a leader? You are a leader only if people follow you."

She took it all in. "Will, I have seen the dumb luck cases of leadership in my volunteering, and you are right, no one wanted to follow them. Actually, come to think of it, the vast majority did everything they could to get away from them."

"Exactly. Once you understand how this works and apply it, you will become a magnet of influence that will move out to others around you and into the organizations you work for and your community, and ultimately it allows you to affect your entire industry to achieve those audacious goals. So, my friend, based on your current and long-term audacious goals, what level of influence is required to achieve that level of audaciousness to realize the goal?"

She was quiet for a moment, wrapping up her ferocious note-taking, and landed her gaze on the audacious goal that was now framed and prominently displayed above the focus space she had made in the corner of her room. She read it out loud: "'To revolutionize the technology and devices used to treat those with diabetes and to advocate prevention.' I added that last part just before I printed it for the wall in my focus space."

He congratulated her, but she remained focused on understanding this concept and pressed on. "So to create the change...I have to be the change? 'I have to be the change' is written in my notes, and it was an earlier answer to something you said, but I feel it is important here. The change, the work, the goals, and the success have to start with me. I have to 'be' it first. Does this make sense?" She quickly answered her own question. "I know that I'm rambling a bit, but I am just talking it through."

"Not a problem, and you're right. It does start with you and 'be the change you wish to see in the world' is a powerful quote by Gandhi that certainly applies here regarding your influence. So, what level of influence will you need in this world?"

She nearly stopped breathing as it hit her. "Will, I am going to have to be the very best in technology, engineering, and biomedical. I must become an expert in them all, and I will also be leading very large groups of people. It will be the only way to get this done. Wow, I chose a really big goal, didn't I?" She spoke these words to herself, to her own heart.

"Yes you did, and I am confident that you will achieve anything you set out to do. But where do we start today?"

She smiled and through a long exhale said, "With leading myself."

"You got it! Now let's take it a few more steps."

She thought they were done and was closing her notebook. "OK." She now rolled her eyes, then caught herself. This is my mentor on the phone. He is giving me this time for free! Guilt instantly set in and she focused back.

Will sensed she needed a boost, so he chose a story for her. "Alexis, your passion for change reminds me of a group I've worked with in Detroit. It is called Focus: HOPE." He paused as if paying silent tribute. "This organization was started in the late sixties to deal with the deep systemic community challenges that Detroit faced at that time. Eradicating the racial division, hunger, economic disparities, and inadequate education was their audacious goal. Forty-five years later, they are renowned experts, known for their fruit. They have campuses that offer vocational STEM programs where they have trained and transitioned tens of thousands into successful careers, fed tens of millions through their food program, and transformed surrounding neighborhoods into villages of hope.

"I have been there and seen firsthand the huge impact they have made in the lives of millions in the Detroit area and beyond. But let's consider that forty-five years ago, they had to start somewhere. They were right where you are today. This organization didn't just happen, it required that they climb their own hill of potential to become kinetic. I guarantee that it has been quite a roller-coaster ride for them over the years."

Alexis pictured the faces of the kinds of people this organization was impacting one by one: young, old, black, white, yellow, red, boys, girls. "Alexis," Will said, and she snapped back to the present. "How will you start to grow your own leadership skills to be this impactful and influential?"

She scrambled a bit. "I can look for ways to lead in one of the student organizations. Be better prepared for my classes and labs so that I can help others. I also need to learn more about the career field I am going into, so I can speak to the problems better."

"I agree with joining student organizations to practice your leadership skills. It will be a safe environment and is designed to do so, quite frankly. The rest that you mentioned are great ways to grow your ability to influence. I would like to suggest a couple of additional ways you can develop your leadership skills specifically."

She wrote "Leadership Skills" on a new page. "OK, go ahead. I'm ready!"

"Just like in school, you can learn any subject matter by studying it. Leadership is the same. There are some books that have been instrumental to me, and you should check them out: *21 Irrefutable Laws of Leadership*, by John Maxwell, *The Truth About Leadership*, by James M. Kouzes and Barry Z. Posner, and *The Servant Leader*, by Ken Blanchard. I have found that the audio versions of these types of books can be helpful. It rests your eyes and you can take in the content quickly.

"The next is volunteering, which you are so passionate about. It's said that when one gives, one also receives. This concept becomes truly visible when one volunteers time in one's community, not to mention how beneficial it is to the nonprofit organizations, the people served by the nonprofits, and the volunteer herself. Oftentimes when volunteering, you'll have the opportunity to develop many different skills, like public speaking, project management, interpersonal relationships, leadership, and, most important, collaboration. Granted, this environment can be quite challenging and complex, but you can really sharpen your leadership skills there."

This was an area where Alexis had firsthand experience. "As you know, I have volunteered quite a bit over the years, and I never thought about the skills I have developed during the process. This is good stuff! Is there more?"

"Yes. Over the past couple of months you have been my mentee and, believe it or not, I have learned a lot from our conversations. I would encourage you to consider mentoring someone in the near future."

This stunned her. "Wow! You have learned things from working with me? But I don't think I'm ready to mentor someone right now, and my time is so limited." She felt confident that she'd successfully shot the topic down, as she had no desire to mentor just then.

"Have you ever tutored someone in a subject such as math or chemistry?"

Dang it, he came back. "Oh yeah. I did that a couple of times when I was working on my first degree."

He pressed further. "While you were helping that other person, did you find that you became better at the subject?"

She was beginning to understand. "I did. I often felt that as she learned, I also learned."

"Exactly! That's the same thing that happens when you mentor someone. You don't have to become a mentor just yet, but I want you have it on your radar as something to participate in."

She raised her hands in surrender. "OK, OK. I can agree to that."

"Good. Now at the beginning of our conversation today, I mentioned that developing your influence skills is a lifelong process. We will be discussing the influence skills during future conversations so keep it on your radar. In conclusion, Alexis, you know that this would not be a mentoring session without a couple of action items for you."

"I know. I was waiting for them."

He smiled. "Good, you are getting used to my madness." They both laughed. "Yes, I think I am!"

He looked down at his watch and moved ahead quickly. "As I mentioned earlier, your ability to influence and lead others begins with self-leadership. I want you to think about the level of discipline you will need to accomplish your audacious goal. Next, what methods will you use to hold yourself accountable? Lastly, since leadership is a skill we have to develop daily, what will be the first skill you will focus on developing?"

She cut in, "Will, I understand the first two action items, but can you expand on the last one?"

"Yes, no problem. Being a strong leader requires mastery of a wide set of skills, and some of those skills are communication, the ability to delegate, strategic thinking, envisioning the future, being a developer of talent, systems thinking, et cetera. Do you follow me now?"

She thought about it for a couple of heartbeats. "I understand. There isn't just one skill that makes a good leader, it's an accumulation of skills?"

He said, smirking, "Bingo! What has she won, Bob?" Laughter erupted between them as they said their goodbyes.

Influence – Homework

- What level of influence is required to achieve your audacious goals?
  - What are the leadership skills that you must develop to achieve that level of influence?
  - Create a plan to grow these skills.
- Who in your circle of influence would benefit from your mentoring?
  - Initiate the mentoring conversation with that person.
- How will you hold yourself accountable to reaching your audacious goals?

Notes:

_____

_____

_____

_____

_____

_____

_____

_____

_____

_____

_____

_____

_____

_____

_____

_____

_____

Part III
Body

CHAPTER 6

Action

Roller Coaster of Life

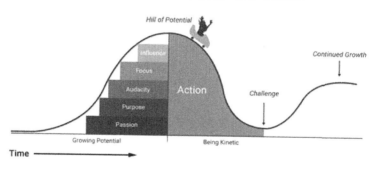

"I can't believe it has been a month since we've talked! Time is flying by with this hectic pace. How are you doing? Did you have a good holiday weekend?" Alexis sounded chaotic, which had become a common occurrence lately.

"I had a great weekend. Rosa and I took our boys, Martin and Miles, to the state fair. They had a blast riding the rides and eating fair food. Martin tried fried Twinkies and Miles had fried pineapple upside-down cake."

"Mmm, that sounds good. What did you have?"

"Tums. I got heartburn just looking at all that fried food. What about you? How are things going?"

"I have been busy, busy, busy. I just finished my first round of exams and am still managing to work twenty-five to thirty hours on my nights and weekends. I know getting this degree will help me achieve my goals, but it still feels like I'm not making progress. Does that make sense?"

"I understand where you're coming from. What you're experiencing is normal when you're in the trenches. The good news is that this happens to be what we will be talking about today, focused action. I'll help you create a plan of action that will measure your results and encourage you."

This hit Alexis unexpectedly. She hadn't realized that she was holding onto discouragement. "That would be helpful, because when I finished my exams and slowed down"—she searched for the words—"I felt overwhelmed with emotion. So, encouragement? I am ready for it!"

"Well, I spoke to two of my mentees, Winnie and Nelson, last week on a group call. Winnie reminds me of you. She has always been passionate about two things in life, learning about nature and science, particularly when it pertains to environmental topics, and giving back to her community by volunteering.

"It was around 2011, when she was pursuing a degree in environmental engineering, that she had the opportunity to volunteer on a water project for a rural village in Central America. This was a great experience for her, because the position was on the engineering team and it allowed her to combine two passions, engineering and volunteering. It profoundly reshaped how she views the world and gave her insight into how she could make a difference. You see, it's Winnie's belief that all people should have access to clean, healthy drinking water. This belief became her passion and fueled her up the hill of potential. She ultimately created an organization that provides clean drinking water to people around the world. Much like you, while she was climbing the hill she went to school and worked. The only difference is that her job was with a water-processing company. This directly aligned with her goal and gave her much-needed experience, but she had to focus on finding a specific job that served her in this way."

"Wow, she's got it all together. Seems like everyone has it together but me. I sometimes get frustrated because so many of my friends have graduated and gone on to great jobs—taking vacations, even starting families. Me, I am back in school and working in a coffee shop." Sarcasm entered her voice through her self-defeating thoughts.

Will was quick to correct her. "Alexis, how many of these people do you maintain a close relationship with?"

She thought about it. "Actually, none of them. I only see what they post." She instantly knew the point he was making.

"Not everyone has their crap together, Alexis. We are in a modern-day land of make-believe called social media. Not to say it is all false or faked, but most of the time it leaves the wrong impression that people have it all together, when in reality they don't. No one really does. Even

Winnie had serious doubts, but she pushed through, with a little help."

"With your help?"

Will smiled. "Yes, I was a champion along with others. Remember, Alexis, I am going to push you just like I did Winnie to get you to your audacious goals."

"I like that you push me and appreciate your support. It has made a huge difference in my life. Come think of it, when I talk to my friends about our sessions, they seem to need this kind of support also. I guess there are a lot more of us in transition than meets the eye."

He leaned back in his chair, knowing that there were a lot more in need of this kind of help. "Yes, like I mentioned in the first session we had, we are *all* on the roller coaster called life." He took in a deep breath, recalling their first meeting and how far they'd come since.

"So, moving on"—he was steering out of the nostalgia and back to the agenda—"did you think about your influence skills? The action items were about self-leadership?"

"Yes, when I thought more about self-discipline, I realized how important my time management is right now. So I started a daily to-do list and am holding myself accountable to getting all the items accomplished each day."

Will chimed in, "I will be holding you accountable for that."

"I would really appreciate the extra accountability, because even I can creatively procrastinate." She laughed softly at her own joke. "By doing the homework, I have realized that I lack an important leadership skill, communication. I get so nervous when I have to speak in front of people, and

I know that my goals will not be accomplished if I keep sharing my vision with one person at a time. I'd need ten lifetimes to accomplish my goals. So I decided to work on that skill through the biomed organization that I just joined and also take an extra public speaking class at school."

"That sounds like a great plan. It seems to me that you are now ready for the next level up in your hill of potential. If we go back to the diagram, you understand that when a roller coaster reaches the summit of the first hill, it has reached its full potential. Then, as it crests over the top, it becomes kinetic. That kind of conversion of potential to kinetic is the same for all of us. You can see on the diagram that our conversations up to this point focused on maximizing the potential in your heart and head. Going forward, we will use this to take the actions required to move you kinetically toward your audacious goals. This is when your body physically engages all that potential you have built up."

She was confused. "Am I not already engaging my potential?"

"You are. You've taken action steps to climb your hill of potential, and that is exciting to see, but you must focus on taking this action each and every day with this momentum behind you. You need to understand that reaching the top of our hill of potential is wonderful, but it takes action to achieve our goals. If we don't act, our potential will just sit idle. We must continuously move forward or our potential will be sadly wasted. We've all met those people who have a huge amount of potential in them, but for some reason they avoid activating it."

"Yes, I have, and I agree it is very sad. But why is that? What stops them?"

He didn't hesitate in giving a very direct response. "Fear. It is the one thing I have observed over these many years of working with people that can become the greatest barrier. It blocks people from taking action. Fear can rear its ugly head in many ways, and we all experience fear at some point."

She challenged him. "You don't experience fear anymore, do you?"

"Of course I do. It is a natural human instinct. The good news is that when we do experience it, we can also arm ourselves to combat it. One fear I have struggled with is fear of the unknown. It would come out in my negative self-talk, which often would come from a conversation with someone that would plant a seed of doubt in my mind. I would use phrases that start with 'what if.' What if I don't succeed, or what if I'm not good enough? Then I heard Zig Ziglar speak on campus when I was in college. He said, 'FEAR is False Evidence Appearing Real.' He was right, and since then I speak to my own fear, asking is it real or is it false? If it is real, what is the evidence? Most of the time the answers would came back false and I was only reacting emotionally to circumstances. Had I let that fear perpetuate, take root, and grow within me, it would have slowed me down and wasted the potential I had built. Alexis, you have so much potential, and I do not want to see it wasted with fear. Fear has no weight to hold you down, therefore it has no leverage in your life."

Above all the lessons she was being taught in this process, she felt this lesson deep in her soul, in her gut. Her fears could seem so real. "Wow, that is, well…," she exhaled, "powerful. I think the fear that I am going to fail is the worst one of all. It takes a great deal of my energy when I think about it in this way." Her words were filled with defeat. The fear had become part of her everyday existence and was like a giant weight on her shoulders. She felt sad that she'd not faced this before, yet hopeful that maybe it could now be confronted.

"Fear of failure is a natural occurrence. Think about how babies learn to walk. They have to fail over and over again. The first falls can end up in a face-plant or land them on their backs. Then eventually they use their arms while they're learning to fall forward and their balance increases. That is what walking is, after all, falling forward and catching ourselves one step at a time.

"So you see, failure is a natural event. It is not who we are, but like babies, we learn how to use our failures to create our success. You know the crazy thing about it? Success isn't about never failing, it is about learning how to fail faster. So when we use failure properly, we can take what we learn from our experience to make better decisions.

"Take Thomas Edison, for example. He tried over a thousand different designs for the lightbulb. He knew that all he had to do was find the one that worked. When he was asked about his failure rate, he said that he had simply found a thousand ways that didn't work."

Alexis chimed in, "Now that you bring this up, I can see that even in doing research is all about failing. You eliminate the wrong answers to find the right answers."

"Exactly. So, like in Edison's case, you see that failure is simply the process of elimination. I'm reminded of a time when failure dramatically changed my life. It was when I was a college student and experiencing all the same twists, turns, rises, and falls that you have. I was academically suspended due to a poor GPA in my freshman year and a so-so GPA in my sophomore year. This experience could have crushed my academic career or transformed it."

She was shocked. "What? You, the great and powerful Will, were suspended from college? I would have never guessed that!" He suddenly took on a much more human form for her, and she responded unreservedly, "I thought you just breezed through college and up the ladder in the corporate world!"

He was amused by her reaction. "Oh, no. Like a favorite poem of mine called 'Mother to Son' by Langton Hughes says, 'life for me ain't been no crystal stair.' Now, during this time I was pushed by my parents, because they believed that you either work or go to school. In some cases, you do both. Therefore, sitting around my parents' house was not an option after the suspension."

She knew this story well. "Your parents sound a lot like my parents."

"Yes, they do. So within a couple of weeks of returning home, I was blessed to secure two part-time jobs. One job was working the concession stands at the local arena and the second job was unloading trucks for a shipping company every day from noon to four. Understand, these trucks sat in the Texas heat all morning, turning them into ovens that would bake me. The pain I experienced when unloading those trucks made me realize I could not do this the rest of my life. It forced me to shift my attitude back toward my education, and I could no longer merely attend college. I'd have to focus on being the best student I could possibly be. So to make that transformation, I learned how to learn. I attended workshops and read books on how to study, and also learned how to connect with my professors and the university staff to get help along the way.

"When I returned to college that fall, I was a new student. I changed my major to mechanical engineering, changed who I associated with, and realigned myself toward who I wanted to be. The great thing is, three years later, I graduated with an engineering degree and was employed as an engineer right out of college, which was significant, because just like today, it was a very tough job market.

"What made it an over-the-top rags-to-riches story came nine years later, when I received a phone call from my alma mater. They were asking me if I would consider becoming a board member of the college of engineering and science. My answer was, of course, yes. However, at the first board meeting, when we were reviewing the documents for maintaining their accreditation"—Will's voice became animated—"it was so ironic. I'd come from being kicked out to helping them stay ahead in the game."

"You have had many twists and turns on your roller coaster too! It makes me feel a bit more normal." She sat back in her chair and relaxed a bit. "Weren't you worried about what they, you know, the board, would say about your suspension?" Alexis often worried what others thought but gave the appearance that she didn't.

"I never brought it up. They knew my academic history, or at least had access to it. I finished strong despite my fumble early on, and that, apparently, was what mattered. That brings us to another fear that derails so many. The fear of 'they' or 'them.' Do you ever ask yourself, 'What are they going to say if I do this or don't do that?'"

She didn't reply.

Will continued, "The thing we have to realize is that people are going to talk regardless of what we do in life. If we do something great or something small, people will talk. Let them talk, because you have bigger things to accomplish. Unfortunately, we live in a culture that spends an inordinate amount of time fixated on gossip. Just look at your cable guide and the number of TV shows focused on what movie stars, politicians, and athletes are doing on a daily basis, and please don't get me started on reality TV." She could hear his brows furrowing. "Now stand back and take a good look at those who are sucked into it. The chance that these people will overcome this to experience audacious success in their lives has been dramatically altered."

"Will, this is so true. I have watched this happen to people around me, and even though I am not much on watching that kind of TV, it still manages to seep in through others. It's like that seed gets planted, and it's an epidemic with people these days."

"Well put. This culture does create a fear of living out our full potential. Realizing we have the power to change the world can be a terrifying moment. Often society reinforces the emotion and causes us to be even more afraid." Will paused for a moment. "I'm reminded of a passage by Marianne Williamson from her book *A Return to Love* that I keep on my desk: 'Our deepest fear is not that we are inadequate. Our deepest fear is that we are powerful beyond measure. It is our light, not our darkness, that most frightens us....And as we let our own light shine, we unconsciously give other people permission to do the same. As we are liberated from our own fear, our presence automatically liberates others.'

"You see, courage is acting despite having fear. So, Alexis, what is your biggest fear that could potentially hold you back from taking action toward your audacious goals?"

She sat deep in thought with the quote, and his question snapped her back. "Wow, that was deep. Um...well... first of all, I don't think that I struggled too much with fear. But now I realize that my old fears have become normal and new fears have become a new normal. I don't want any of this to be my normal." She paused to reset. "I am afraid that I will get this degree and fail to find a job again."

Will grinned empathetically at her valid response. "I understand that your history tells you to fear this. Why let it slow you down or stop you from working toward your dream, your audacious goals?"

She responded, with full transparency, "I'm also afraid I will not have enough fuel in my tank to get me where I want to go."

He leaned into the phone. "Do you have enough to get started, Alexis?"

She looked up as if to heaven. "Yes."

He confidently pressed in. "Good. Then keep going with the fuel you have now, which I know is sufficient. We will figure out how to refill the tank later. I want you to keep something in mind: by removing fear, you will gain lots of mileage out of that same amount of fuel."

"OK, that seems so simple to me. I feel like my tank just filled up!" Her voice carried the rays of hope she felt in her spirit.

"Good, you are going to need it for all you have going on. Truth be told, everyone is entrenched in activities, but to reach your audacious goals, you have to push harder in the specific areas that drive you toward that goal. You must be willing to get into the grind and make them your reality. So tell me, what specific daily actions are you going to take today toward obtaining your audacious goal?"

Alexis thought a moment "Isn't that my to-do list? Which, honestly, is more than I can accomplish in a day. It seems unrealistic." Her voice trailed off.

"Well, my friend, nothing great happens without sweat and hard work. I suggest that you create thirty-, sixty-, ninety-day plans in addition to a daily to-do list. It might seem overwhelming at first, but in your journal you should start with the big goals for this year. After that, break it down into semesters and then into months. This will give you the next three months of plans so you can measure your progress. It is important to know where you are in relation to the goal. It helps you to build and keep momentum.

"One of the best ways to ensure that you are writing solid goals is to use the SMART criteria.

Specific: define what you are trying to do.
Measurable: can you quantify the results you seek?
Achievable: can you really do this?
Relevant: does this support your bigger goal?
Time-based: when do you want to complete this goal?

"So your plan might include additional research, developing those communications skills we talked about, maybe meeting new people in your industry using social media resources like LinkedIn or joining groups that support your goal."

"My mind is a whirlwind of thoughts. So where do I start to eat this elephant?"

He picked up what she was putting down. "One bite at a time. That is the law of small things. I remember one month I made a goal of doing fifteen hundred pushups, as a personal health challenge."

She was surprised. "Dang, that is a lot of pushups! Did you do it?"

His reply had a distinctive hint of sarcasm. "Of course I did! I know fifteen hundred pushups sounds like a lot, but it's not if you break it up in small parts. For one month, I did a minimum of fifty pushups a day, and at the end of the month I had actually surpassed my goal with over seventeen hundred pushups. So, you see, if you come up with manageable daily goals, they will take you day by day toward that larger goal."

"You know, I like to be organized and feel that I am accomplishing something every day toward my dreams. This will definitely help me do that. Our hour is almost up. Homework?"

He liked that question. "Absolutely. Identify one or two activities you can do on a daily basis that will help you achieve your larger thirty-, sixty-, ninety-day goals. Send me a summary of what those are, but be detailed for yourself, because being a great leader is to be self-led, as we've talked about. It isn't proven when others are watching, but when they aren't. Your self-discipline will only have a contingency of one, you."

Her response hit the nail on the head. "I see. What you are saying is that I might have a big tribe, but I have to push myself because I will fail from time to time. It is up to me to fall forward and maintain my drive in order to achieve the success of my audacious goals. My dreams."

They ended the call and Will leaned back in his chair, deep in thought. This was why he mentored. The mentees got so much from the sessions, and so did he. Alexis was special, she had incredible potential, and now she was becoming empowered to achieve anything she set out to do. All it took was a little guidance and, as the song goes, a little help from her friends.

Action – Homework

- Create your thirty-, sixty-, and ninety-day plans.
- Create a daily to-do list with specific activities.
- Identify one or two daily activities that will help you achieve your larger thirty-, sixty-, and ninety-day goals.

Notes:

Part IV
Staying Kinetic

CHAPTER 7

Staying Kinetic

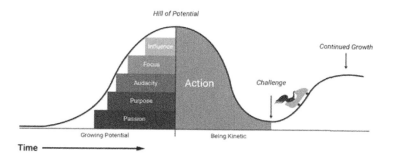

Roller Coaster of Life

Hill of Potential

Influence

Focus

Audacity

Action

Purpose

Passion

Continued Growth

Challenge

Growing Potential

Being Kinetic

Time

lexis settled into her focus space at home and pulled out her journal with the action items from their last session three weeks ago. While the past weeks were still busy, the process of mapping her goals had done wonders for her energy level and daily satisfaction. She was now measuring her accomplishments, and seeing them in black and white reminded her of what she was capable of accomplishing.

<u>Leadership Skill to Develop:</u>
Communication with a focus on public speaking.
<u>Daily Actions:</u>
- Contribute more in class discussions.
- Seek a role in the biomed organization that will require me to speak to groups.

<u>Quarterly Goal:</u>
Learn more about where the biomedical industry is heading.
<u>Thirty-day Goal:</u>
Learn more about the biomedical industry in the Northwest.
- Create a list of biomed companies in the NW.
- Find out which of these companies recruit at my university.

<u>Sixty-day Goal:</u>
List the Biomed research being conducted at my university.
- Talk with the dean of the biomed department about new research programs.
- Talk with professors about research they are conducting.
- Meet with John for help.

<u>Ninety-day Goal:</u>
Understand the top trends in the biomed industry.
- Identify top jobs in demand today.
- Identify top future research areas.
- Learn more about areas of highest impact for treating diabetes.

The last bullet point brought her back to the beginning, her 'why': Devi. She thought about all that had changed since she started the Kinetic Life process, which moved her onto this amazing life path.

Since her first meeting with Will, Alexis had been sharing her journey with Devi and the results had been remarkable. Devi had begun to see past the tragic circumstances and was focusing on her own passions, purpose, and goals in life.

Alexis sat back and realized that she had been paying it forward, not just with Devi, but with many of her friends and classmates. She was told quite often lately that her light was shining bright and it encouraged others. It was a ripple effect, like dropping a pebble into water, the ripples go out to impact all that is around you. A chill ran up her spine and she said aloud, "This is really awesome."

■ ■ ■

"How's one of my favorite mentees today? The last time we talked, you seemed stressed with all that is going on in your world."

Alexis rolled her eyes. "That was so last month! Things are a lot better and I can report that I have survived the storm. There is so much I want to tell you. I almost sent you a text but wanted to share it with you face-to-face—well, voice-to-voice."

"This sounds like a huge shift. Please, tell me more."

Trying to contain herself, she took a deep breath. "I found a new job! After all these years I am FINALLY going to work doing something that I am passionate about. I am beyond excited!"

"Excellent, Alexis, congrats on the new gig! I'm glad to hear you're in your zone. So tell me, how did you find the job?"

"Thank you so much! It was the homework you gave me in our last session. You told me to create thirty-, sixty-, and ninety-day plans and to focus on a leadership skill that I needed to develop, and I did. So one of the items on my thirty-day plan was to learn more about the biomed companies here in the Northwest, and there was a company close to me that caught my eye, BioTECH. As I looked through their website, I found out they were scheduled to be on campus the next week to recruit."

"That is really incredible!"

Alexis instantly responded, "That's just the beginning. We had our biomed group monthly meeting the night before, so I asked our chapter president if I could invite the recruiter to speak, and he was cool with it. I emailed the recruiter directly, and she not only accepted the invitation, but was excited about the opportunity. We spoke on the phone a couple of days before to go over the details of the meeting and how she would like to be introduced to the group, which I will be doing. Will, it happened so fast. One minute we are talking about the speech and the next she was asking me about my career goals! I had no idea that she was interviewing me as a candidate for a part-time position within their new U-sourcing program on campus. What was scheduled for fifteen minutes went on for forty-five. It went so well. What can I say, we just clicked!"

"Sounds like it was a great conversation and great timing! Now this program, U-source, what is it?"

Alexis was well prepared to share. "It's a concept that was new to me as well. It is similar to outsourcing, but instead of recruiting employees from outside the company and often from outside the US, these companies open small offices on college campuses where students can work part time. That way, when you graduate you'll have a better understanding of what career path you might want to take within a company, and in most circumstances the student is hired full time. But you want to know the coolest part? The pay is really good, I'll get some benefits and most of all I will be getting that real work experience we talked about!"

He loved the enthusiasm. "Sounds like you hit the trifecta to me."

"Yeah! And I will be starting in two weeks, although it was bittersweet when I told Roland at the coffee shop. They have done so much for me over the years. I am really going to miss them, so I offered to help out on Saturdays if they needed me." She quickly moved to her agenda. "OK, now that I've gotten a 'real-world' job, I want to make a great start with this company. Do you have any suggestions for me? Keep in mind that I also don't want to mess with everything else I have going on now. How do you suggest that I keep all this momentum going?"

Will heard her self-leadership blossoming in the line of questioning. "I'm so excited for you. I can feel your energy. Now, let me answer your last question first. Reflecting back on our first conversation at the TAF conference and seeing where you are today, you have certainly built up an epic amount of momentum toward your audacious goals and that, Alexis, is something you should celebrate. It is this momentum that will take you up and over the hills of opposition, and from what I've seen, you'll just smash through the roadblocks."

She came back with humorous sass. "So you think I'm epic?"

"That you are. You must keep in mind that when facing these future challenges, each can become another opportunity to build your potential. So when you face a new challenge, I recommend that you first do a heart check. You need to verify that your passion, purpose, and audacity are still in alignment with your current direction. If they aren't, then you must make the necessary adjustments. After that, check what's in your head and determine where you need to turn your focus to solve the current challenges. Finally, understand the influence that will be needed to put your solution into play."

She looked at the image of the roller coaster on her desk. "I think I've got it. So you are saying the roller coaster of life repeats itself?"

"Yes, it does. Now understand that there is a skill that's often overlooked and it will help you overcome future roadblocks, and it's your attitude. In life, you can't control all the circumstances you'll face. What we can control is our attitude toward those events.

"I remember many years ago, the company I was working for went through a round of layoffs. As I talked with a few who were impacted, I found it amazing that some felt it was the worst day of their career and others felt it was the most liberating. One woman I distinctly remember talking with was laid off yet excited about the new opportunities ahead of her. She told me that she'd been discussing moving back to the east coast with her husband for quite some time, and being laid off provided the perfect opportunity to do it. So some people look at such an issue or challenge as a growth opportunity, while others see issues or roadblocks from a point of despair. Part of the reason for their despair is that ugly four-letter word again, fear. Don't let it creep in and stop you. Don't let it steal your joy. Instead, you just keep on pushing."

"That makes so much sense. I have seen both sides of this in how I have responded to Devi's circumstances. At first it put the entire family in a valley of despair, but when my attitude changed, it became my greatest opportunity. Oh! I've not told you. Devi went into a research study and has a leading-edge prosthetic foot! It is unbelievable, and while she's been recovering from the amputation, I taught her most of the Kinetic Life process. Well, to tell the truth, she demanded to know about everything we were working on, and she used the process to look at her own potential."

That struck Will in the heart. "How awesome. And...?"

"Devi is now volunteering at the hospital, working with amputees. Her motto is, 'If I can do it, so can you!' She always follows this up by showing off her high-tech prosthetic."

Will cut in, "Encouragement is one of the biggest gifts we can give someone."

Alexis knew this was true. "It is so great to see her transformation, and it makes me understand why you mentor. It is so inspiring to me. It fills up my tank!"

"Alexis, you are exactly right. Over all these years I have been mentoring, I have discovered that each success, each victory impacts me as if it were my own. Along with the other steps I have taught you, mentoring will be a great source for you. Oh, and hey, congratulations on this and on the new job!"

Alexis felt a great sense of pride. "Thank you. I would not have made it this far without your help!" They both smiled, silently taking in the moment.

"You are welcome. I guess the next thing is to answer your first question, and it had better be good, because you are going to pass it on to Devi."

This drew laughter from Alexis. "I'm ready!"

"All right. Starting a new job is a big step and laying a good foundation is important. Whether you are constructing a house, a monument, or even a skyscraper in a major city, there is one thing that all these structures must have: a solid foundation. Having a solid foundation will enable these structures to stand tall through the various challenges they will face over time. The same goes for your career. So, in starting this new job you can use these steps to build a solid foundation within that organization.

"Step one: understand the direction of the company. The better you understand where your company is going, what its big bets are and where it invests its time and money, the better decisions you will be able to make. When it is time for you to make decisions, you will be able to make the decisions that will strengthen the company's bottom line.

"Step two: know your manager. Knowing your manager provides you with the information you'll need to help determine the best way to work with him or her, meet his or her needs, and stand out by exceeding expectations. While you are getting to know your manager, it is important to understand how his or her goals tie into the company's goals. Something to remember: your manager is often the gatekeeper to your next raise or promotion. So managing this relationship is key.

"Step three: connect with your team. You have heard the saying that nobody works alone? We must rely on our colleagues to produce our best work or to meet the objectives of the organization. Make it an early priority to connect with your teammates.

"As for your long-term career management, YOU have to take ownership of your career. You must have a forward-thinking approach so that you always know how what you are doing fits into your professional future. If you don't do this, you can get stuck in a hurry."

"This goes along with my goal planning? I mean, when I add my new job to my thirty, sixty, ninety planning, it should bring my career into alignment with my goals?"

He liked her observation. "Yes. But I caution you, things can change in the blink of an eye and the change may not fit your plans. Be sure to reassess your long-term goals frequently and make the necessary adjustments to the daily goals when necessary."

She was feverishly taking notes. "Got it."

"In addition, leverage your knowledge of the industry, the company's goals, and the items your manager is responsible for accomplishing. This is how you can identify potential career opportunities.

"Lastly, and this is a critical component, you must always remember that being too comfortable in the workplace is dangerous, so stay in motion. You can't stand still. No matter how much you learn or achieve, it's important to keep moving upward. Alexis, you are very smart and you learn things quickly. Because of those skills, you may become bored with your job, so you must remember there is always something that you can do to mitigate the boredom."

"You know, we have talked about my impatience. May I ask you to hold me accountable in this way? I mean, check in with me from time to time to ask if I feel challenged in my position?"

"Absolutely I will, and feel free to reach out to me anytime you feel you are getting stuck. We will work through it. So once you begin to master your current position, you should seek new opportunities and challenges that will allow you to continue to grow. If you don't and you get too comfortable in your position, you will be in danger of going from having a career to simply having a job."

"How can anyone be productive if it is just a job? There would be no passion, no purpose. Seems like a horrible existence to me."

Will had seen this in companies he consulted all too often. "It is, and similarly, this attitude of being too complacent isn't just detrimental for an employee, it's detrimental to a company, because companies that don't grow don't survive. I remember the stories about Jack Welch when he was CEO of General Electric. He constantly challenged his leaders to find areas in the business where GE was not the market leader. Applying the same principle to your career will force you to constantly seek opportunities where you can grow and learn."

"When you say learn, I think of college. Once I have my degree, should I continue to take courses?" She was slightly confused.

"You can. Like you, I also had a strong desire to be successful, and I knew ongoing learning and training was imperative to achieving this. So a strategy I have used throughout my career was to seek out and attend motivation workshops and trainings that were hosted in my community or at the various engineering and business conferences that I'd attend throughout the year.

"At one of the conferences, a concept really resonated with me. They said that if you want to be successful, you have to apply it. It's called the CANI principle, and it was created by Anthony Robbins. CANI stands for constant and never-ending improvement, which ultimately means to always seek ways to grow and develop your knowledge, talent, and skills. When you look at the truly great leaders in their chosen line of work, they are always striving and looking for ways to get better at what they do. So, Alexis, how can you apply the CANI principle in this new job?"

She paused a moment to think. "Well, the initial learning curve will be significant. After that, and in addition to my course load, I will look into our local STEM and biomed associations for conferences and workshops. I can offer to volunteer in exchange for entry."

He really appreciated her out-of-the-box thinking. "Or in some cases, your company might sponsor your attendance. Remember, the company is investing in your becoming a valued employee. Just approaching your managers with the subject tells them you live by CANI principles. This is a win-win."

"I like it and will approach management after I've had a chance to settle in."

Will looked at his watch. "I'm going to have to hop off here in two minutes. I wanted you to know that in our future conversations we will go deeper into how to have a Kinetic Career. We will be using some of the same principles I've taught you, but with all our energy focused on accelerating your career growth. Is that a deal?"

"Of course it's a deal!" She realized that they had completed the initial round of learning.

"You're going to be stuck with me as a mentor for many years to come, Alexis."

"I'm counting on it."

Immediately after hanging up the phone, she realized he hadn't given her homework. This wasn't right, and she had to keep up the progress. Just as she went to open an email to ask him for it, she saw her notes from the call and knew exactly what she had to do: lead herself.

Staying Kinetic – Homework

- What are some potential roadblocks or challenges you might face?
  - What can you do to prepare for them?
- Where will you apply the CANI principle in your life?
- How will you lead yourself going forward?

Notes:

_____

_____

_____

_____

_____

_____

_____

_____

_____

_____

_____

_____

_____

_____

_____

_____

_____

_____

Conclusion

lexis took her position at the podium and the stage
lighting blinded her from seeing the audience beyond the first rows. She looked down with grati-
tude at the lead table. Her tribe was there. Will and his
wife, Rosa, her parents, Roland and Martha from the coffee
shop and, of course, Devi.

She took a deep breath, calming her heart, and began
her acceptance speech. "Diabetes impacts nearly ten per-
cent of our population, which is a staggering thirty million
people who suffer from this devastating disease. The CDC
reports that last year this came at a cost of two hundred
forty-five billion US dollars and that is expected to rise.

"My personal awareness of the disease came when my
cousin Devi, who's been like a big sister to me and is here
with us today, was diagnosed with type 2 diabetes at age
thirty-two. This disease changed her life forever and the
lives of those closest to her, including my own.

"Shortly after her diagnosis, I was blessed to have my first mentor step into my life. I had completed my degree in marine biology when he invited me to look deep within to find my purpose. I stand before you now to report"—she smiled down at Will and shook her head—"it was not marine biology."

Laughter swept the crowd and Alexis laughed with them. "My mentor labeled me the mad coffee scientist, because after graduation I could not find a job and was working in a coffee shop. As a barista, I applied my love of science to create delectable coffee concoctions, therefore gaining the title.

"This amazing mentor helped me uncover my purpose in life, to produce devices that increase the quality of life for those suffering with this disease. I'm thrilled to announce that with the recent advances of the no-blood wearable glucose-monitoring device, we are right on track.

"Many of you have heard of Will McDowell, author of the bestselling book series *Kinetic*, which to our delight he will be presenting to us on this stage tomorrow. What you may not know is that he was—wait, let me rephrase that, he is my mentor. Will, you haven't just changed my life, you have changed the lives of millions. We all thank you." Sitting at the lead table with praying hands, Will bowed toward Alexis as if to say he was the lucky one. She graciously smiled back at him while the audience applauded.

"I remember the day he pushed me to look past my purpose toward the holy grail of goals to uncover my deepest audacious dreams. I wanted to eradicate diabetes. This answer created an interesting dilemma: the existence of the disease produced the customer for the devices I wanted to provide. I must admit my embarrassment when he pointed it out, but my answer was not wrong.

"Will celebrated the answer by pointing out that my generation, the millennial generation, has a distinct moral compass for the good of humanity. This was where my ethics and values intersected with purpose and contribution. It was that one answer that brought me before you today to accept this prestigious award for the advances made in early-onset education."

After she wrapped up her speech, her friend and moderator came back onstage to allow the audience to ask questions. Alexis felt that ever-present nervousness, which she now channeled to keep focused while onstage.

"Alexis, again, thank you for all you have done in the effort to achieve your audacious goal of eradicating diabetes. While we seek to find a cure, your efforts to educate those who are at highest risk has made a significant difference in the average onset age of this disease. Now let's turn to this over to our audience for questions."

The lights came on, revealing the crowded ballroom. A woman who appeared to be in her late twenties was first up. "You mentioned that Will McDowell mentored you with the Kinetic model. What were the top things you took away from the process?"

"Thank you for that question. I'm always eager to talk about the process, because, as a mentor now myself, I see the power it has to create impactful leaders who will change our world. With that said, my top three? First is the simple fact that there is a process we can follow. Second, it is mandatory that we all have help from our tribe of mentors, teachers, managers, and colleagues. Third, you have to focus on your goals, no matter what oppositions you face."

A young man stepped up to the microphone. "Hi, my question for you is, what was the hardest opposition you faced in achieving this level of success?"

She looked directly into her fellow millennial's eyes. "My own fears, and there were more than I like to admit. The good news is that once you are able to recognize that those fears are fallacies, you can break free of them. It is amusing to me that public speaking was a fear I faced and overcame, but I had to take risks and put myself out there." The gentleman stood for a moment, deep in his own thoughts, until he remembered where he was and proceeded back to his seat.

Alexis answered several scientific and industry-related questions, then the moderator asked, "Last question?"

A young woman took the microphone. "You are the youngest person ever to receive this award, which makes you quite fascinating to many of us who are of your generation. My question might seem prosaic, but it seems to me that your career path to this point has been a straight line. Have you, like many of us, been thrown any curve balls? Can you give us any advice on how to deal with them?"

"Of course I have. It is not about the situation, it is about your response to it. I remember my first full-time job was with a new device company that recruited me straight out of college. The job aligned perfectly with my talents and what I wanted to accomplish. I moved up the ranks quickly, however, the company—and the economy, for that matter—took a downturn and went out of business. We all are aware that this happens often in our industry, especially for companies that take risks in business to solve big problems. This was the case, and my heart was broken over it because I cared so much for the work and the people. The situation forced me to reevaluate what was in my heart and to refocus on my goals."

She paused in reflection. "Two things happened. First, I was incredibly encouraged by taking time to review how far I'd come, and second, I realized that the skills, experience, and talent I had were underutilized at that company. You see, I was so focused on the day-to-day activities that I lost sight of the big picture. So I rewrote my goals, resume, and new daily action items that would push me to the result I sought. I fully admit that I was thrown for a loop, but I applied what Will taught me and took the steps to ascend another hill of potential that has brought me here today. My advice to you is to be your own leader. Become an expert in your own life first and build the skills you need to overcome the hills of opposition long before they enter into your journey. I assure you that by doing this, just as I did, you will go further in life"—Alexis lifted a sweeping hand, pointing out her position in the grand space—"than you could have ever imagined."

Back at the table, Alexis proposed a toast. "Mom, Dad, Devi, Roland, Martha, Rosa, and of course Will, none of this would have happened if it were not for your love, support, and belief in me." She placed the award in the center of the table. "This is our award. I raise my glass to each of you and to the journey ahead. May we continue to reach our maximum potential within so we can rise to new heights and tackle all that is in store for us on this glorious roller coaster called life!"

About the Author

Melerick "Mel" Mitchell believes we all have both the power and the obligation to influence the world for the better.

Mel's Kinetic career focuses on helping companies, teams, and individuals build powerful identities that will change the world.

In 2009, Mel founded Drive Influence to serve current executives as well as their rising talent, teams, and organizations in a wide range of industries, including startups, NGOs, governments, and corporations, to accelerate performance through applying his Kinetic philosophies.

Before launching Drive Influence, Mel worked for ten years at Microsoft in roles that included systems analyst and program manager, and ultimately, he transitioned into a talent development consultant, a unique shift for an engineer and analyst. Mel thrived in this role as he created the Microsoft IT Talent Development Program, which focused on developing the next generation of leaders.

Mel then created, implemented, and managed Microsoft IT's Accelerated Professional Experiences Program (APEX), a two-year global rotational program for new college hires. In addition to managing the APEX program, he led Microsoft IT's High Potential Program, which encompassed driving the selection process for identifying and guiding future leaders through the program's development processes and curriculum.

Mel is passionate about serving his community by volunteering and has served on several nonprofit boards in Dallas, Seattle, Tucson, and Las Vegas. He served as the 2014–2015 National Professionals Chair for the National Society of Black Engineers (NSBE), and he is a past officer of the Dallas chapter of the Association of Talent Development, formerly ASTD. Mel has also developed and facilitated career readiness and leadership programs for organizations such as the Technology Access Foundation in Seattle, Dream Jamaica in Kingston, Jamaica, Tuskegee University, Louisiana Tech University, and Ashesi University in Accra, Ghana.

Mel holds a B.S. in Electrical Engineering Technology from Louisiana Tech University and an M.S. in Electrical Engineering from the University of Nevada, Las Vegas. He has also attended executive educational courses taught at the University of Michigan's Ross School of Business and the University of California, Los Angeles, Anderson School of Management. Mel has also worked as an engineer for Bechtel Nevada and Raytheon Missile Systems.

Roller Coaster of Life

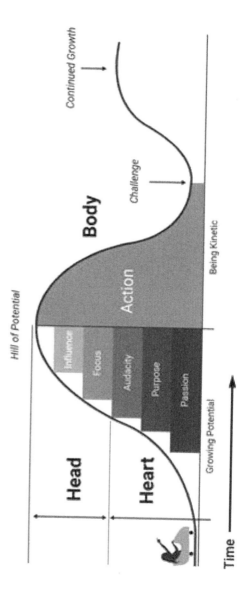

Kinetic Life begins the moment we take action toward our audacious goals in life and it requires alignment of our **Heart, Head** and **Body**.

Building Your Potential	Being Kinetic
Heart – Passion, purpose and audacity provide the fuel for our motivation in life.	**Body** – Specific actions we conduct to move us toward achieving our audacious goals.
Passion – Our heart's internal force that drives us forward in life and is the foundation for our motivation.	Action – Taking action toward our audacious goals is the moment we become Kinetic; it is the leveraging of our potential that moves us forward.
Purpose – The belief in our soul of why we have our particular passion and what we should do with it.	
Audacity – Audacious goals represent the impact we are striving to make.	**Staying Kinetic** – Once in motion we must stay in motion regardless of the resistance we encounter.
Head – Directing our focus and influence will shape the quality of our outcome.	Attitude – The proper mindset necessary to push through the resistance, roadblocks and fear encountered on our journey.
Focus – Concentrating on developing the knowledge required to realize your audacious goal.	Continuous Improvement – The constant striving to be better at our life's calling.
Influence – The leadership skills required to achieve your audacious goal.	

Made in the USA
Middletown, DE
18 July 2022

69639456R00086